REPUBLIC OF IRELAND
On This Day

REPUBLIC OF IRELAND
On This Day

*History, Facts & Figures
from Every Day of the Year*

STEVE MENARY

REPUBLIC OF IRELAND
On This Day

History, Facts & Figures from Every Day of the Year

All statistics, facts and figures are correct as of 1st August 2010

© Steve Menary
Steve Menary has asserted his rights in accordance with the Copyright, Designs and Patents Act 1988 to be identified as the author of this work.

Published By:
Pitch Publishing (Brighton) Ltd
A2 Yeoman Gate
Yeoman Way
Durrington
BN13 3QZ

Email: info@pitchpublishing.co.uk
Web: www.pitchpublishing.co.uk

First published 2010

A catalogue record for this book is available from the British Library.

13-digit ISBN: 978-1-9054118-4-9

Printed and bound in Great Britain by CPI Mackays, Chatham ME5 8TD

To Lesley, Lucie & Scott

ACKNOWLEDGEMENTS

Thanks to the staff of Ringwood Library for their help in sourcing books and to David Barber at the Football Association and Remco Van Dam for their help in providing photos.

A number of books were particularly useful in writing this book, notably Bill Samuel's *The Complete Republic of Ireland FC 1926–2008*, Clive Leatherdale's excellent book *Ireland: The Quest for the World Cup* and *Football Association of Ireland 75 Years* by Peter Byrne.

A full list of all the books and other sources used in the compiling of this book are listed at the end.

INTRODUCTION

Despite having a shorter history than many international teams, the Republic of Ireland has produced enough feats, many heroics, and plenty of fine players to rival or outdo many larger countries. Football has a long, rich heritage in southern Ireland but this book is confined to the footballing activities of the players and team that has been known over the years variously as the Irish Free State, Eire and more latterly the Republic of Ireland.

Since those beginnings in the early 1920s, Ireland have been to the quarter-finals at every significant senior international tournament. After making the last eight of the Olympic Games in their senior bow, Ireland emulated this feat in the European Nations Cup by the 1960s, did so again in the 1980s and then enjoyed success at the finals of three World Cups.

Ireland's transformation over the past few decades at senior level is mirrored by a growing level of international achievement from Irish youth teams, more latterly of both genders.

This is testament to the talent and determination of everyone involved in football in a country where the sport faces heavy competition from rugby union and the Gaelic sports but has shown that having a relatively small population does not prevent international success.

Steve Menary

REPUBLIC OF IRELAND
On This Day

JANUARY

SATURDAY 1st JANUARY 1983

A stand-out performance from their young Republic of Ireland goalkeeper Packie Bonner enables Glasgow Celtic to beat old rivals Rangers at Ibrox Park Stadium for the first time since 1921. "I have never seen Bonner in such form," says Rangers' boss John Greig to *The Times*. "His was a World Cup display."

WEDNESDAY 1st JANUARY 2003

Paddy Daly, who passed away today aged 85, won his only Ireland cap in his country's first World Cup victory, a 3-0 pasting of Finland – replacing the injured Brendan Carroll – despite substitutes being banned in World Cup fixtures. Two months later, Daly left Shamrock Rovers and the League of Ireland (LOI) for Aston Villa but failed to make an impact and dropped out of senior football.

WEDNESDAY 2nd JANUARY 1985

Ipswich reveal that Republic of Ireland winger Kevin O'Callaghan, the Suffolk club's most expensive ever signing, is having talks with Sheffield United. O'Callaghan was signed by Ipswich in 1980 from Millwall for £250,000.

FRIDAY 3rd JANUARY 1986

Des Casey says that Mark Lawrenson and Eoin Hand have applied for the vacant Irish manager's job but the Football Association of Ireland (FAI) president is not taking any more applications. Billy McNeilll, Liam Tuohy and Jack Charlton are the only three names on the FAI's shortlist – for now…

WEDNESDAY 3rd JANUARY 1973

Johnny Giles is the Republic's sole representative in a match at Wembley staged to celebrate Ireland, Denmark and the United Kingdom's entry into what was then known as the Common Market. The match is described as The Three versus The Six, the latter describing the half dozen existing members of the Common Market. England manager Alf Ramsey selects the home team, which also features Pat Jennings from Northern Ireland, Colin Bell of England, Peter Lorimer of Scotland and Henning Jensen of Denmark. The visitors' line-up includes Franz Beckenbauer, Berti Vogts and Ruud Krol. The Three win 2-0 with goals from Henning Jensen of Denmark and Scotland's Colin Stein.

THURSDAY 4TH JANUARY 1951

Paddy Roche, who was born today, was a talented goalkeeper who won eight caps for Ireland over a four-year spell. Roche was still playing in the LOI for Shelbourne when he made his international debut in a scratch team assembled by Liam Tuohy that was thumped 6-0 by Austria. The next year, Manchester United signed Roche for £15,000 but he was generally an understudy to Alex Stepney and Gary Bailey and left in 1982 on a free transfer to Brentford. In his first full season with Brentford, Roche played as many first XI games as he had done in nine years at United.

WEDNESDAY 5TH JANUARY 1972

The Irish Olympic side beat their West German counterparts 3-0 in a friendly.

SATURDAY 6TH JANUARY 1951

Ireland's amateur team play the English for the first time but go down 1-0 in a friendly in Dublin. England also played amateur internationals in Dublin in 1906 and 1908 but that was against an Irish side drawn from the whole island of Ireland.

MONDAY 6TH JANUARY 1986

Paul McShane is born in Kilpedder. He is playing for St Joseph's Boys AFC when he is signed by Manchester United. McShane fails to make the first team but wins Irish under-21 honours. He leaves Old Trafford for West Bromwich Albion, where he becomes a regular and wins the first of many full caps for Ireland, later playing for Brighton, Sunderland and Hull City.

WEDNESDAY 7TH JANUARY 2009

The Irish women's team start the year with their highest world ranking of 27.

TUESDAY 8TH JANUARY 1985

Sheffield United ditched an attempt to sign Ireland winger Kevin O'Callaghan for £100,000 from Ipswich Town. "He was not prepared to take a drop in money to come here," Sheffield manager Ian Porterfield tells *The Times*. "We have a wage structure at the club so the deal is off."

FRIDAY 8TH JANUARY 1982

"Ours is a bad draw but it could have been a lot worse," sighs Ireland manager Eoin Hand to *The Times* after his team are put together with Spain, the Netherlands, Iceland and Malta in qualifying group seven for the 1984 European Championships today. "At least we have avoided the Eastern bloc countries [but] good lord, don't talk about the luck of the Irish. Talk about the luck of the English. I'd give my right leg for their group." England are pitched with Hungary, Greece, Denmark and Luxembourg in a seemingly weak group.

TUESDAY 9TH JANUARY 1962

Ray Houghton, who was born today in Glasgow, is one of Ireland's most capped players with 73 appearances for the Irish XI. An industrious midfielder, he only scores six goals but those strikes include Ireland's first goal in a major finals as England are vanquished 1-0 at Euro 88. Houghton also scored the goal that upset Italy 1-0 at the 1994 World Cup in New York. He started his career at West Ham, where chances are scarce. He joins Fulham, then Oxford United, before spending five seasons at Liverpool, making more than 150 appearances. He later turns out for Aston Villa, Crystal Palace and Reading. When he retires in May 2000, after a handful of appearances for Stevenage Borough, Houghton converts into a regular television pundit for a number of channels, including RTÉ. In 2005 he is given an honorary degree by the University of Huddersfield.

THURSDAY 9TH FEBRUARY 1986

FAI president Des Casey flies to Manchester to meet with the Manchester City chairman to try and recruit Billy McNeill as Ireland's part-time manager. Casey offers to recompense City financially if McNeil can be released for between 20 and 30 days a year to look after Ireland. City rejected the FAI offer and McNeill's name was taken off the shortlist of potential new Ireland managers, which narrows to Liam Tuohy and Jack Charlton.

MONDAY 9TH JANUARY 2006

Ireland's most capped player, Steve Staunton, takes over from Brian Kerr as Irish manager. He will be mentored until qualification is over by ex-Barcelona and England manager, Sir Bobby Robson.

WEDNESDAY 10th JANUARY 1980

Coventry City lose interest in David Langan after the Republic of Ireland international fails to turn up for an FA Cup tie between his club Derby County, and Bristol City, the previous Saturday. Coventry's manager Gordon Milne says he no longer wants to sign Langan because of the right-back's "temperament". Langan subsequently signs for Birmingham City, where he stays for four seasons.

FRIDAY 10th JANUARY 1986

An executive committee meeting of the FAI is expected to confirm the appointment of Ireland's new manager but the press is flooded with leaks over the re-entry into the race of Johnny Giles. FAI president Des Casey asks each committee member individually if they are responsible. The meeting breaks up without any agreement on a new manager.

THURSDAY 11th JANUARY 2001

The Republic of Ireland B team have not played a game since 1999 but today turn down a chance to play the German second string in the summer. "Germany were very keen to play us at B level in June but we had to say no because of the World Cup games," explains FAI international committee member Michael Hyland. "It's a pity – but it would have been impossible to assemble a strong enough squad to take on the Germans."

TUESDAY 12th JANUARY 1982

Ireland are shoved down the seedings for the World Cup draw to be held later this week. England have controversially been awarded a top seeding despite not having played in the finals for 12 years, while Ireland – despite finishing a narrow third in the last World Cup qualifiers – are seemingly in the fourth group of seeds.

SATURDAY 13th JANUARY 1990

The Kelly brothers, Ireland's goalkeeping siblings, get to play against each other in a senior match for the only time. Alan is playing for Bury at Gigg Lane. The visitors are Preston North End, whose custodian is Gary Kelly. Their father, Alan Kelly senior, flies from the USA to see the match.

SUNDAY 14TH JANUARY 1979

The birthday of Richard Sadlier, who spent eight years playing in England with Millwall. He scored 17 goals in the 2001/02 season and played in Ireland's 2-0 win over Russia in 2002 but never featured again.

MONDAY 15TH JANUARY 1923

Tommy Eglington is born in Dublin. One of a number of players to play for the Republic and Northern Ireland, he won two FAI Cup winners' medals and the first of 24 caps for the Republic before he signed for Everton in 1946. A speedy winger, he once scored five goals in a match against Doncaster Rovers in 1952. After leaving Goodison Park, he played for Tranmere Rovers, then Cork Hibs. His last Irish cap was in 1955. After leaving football, he ran a butchers shop in his native Dublin. He died on February 18th 2004, aged 81.

THURSDAY 15TH JANUARY 1981

When Doug Livingstone, who passed away today aged 83, took charge of Ireland in 1951, he had the manager's title but not the power to decide who played where. That was still a long way off for the Scot or any of his successors. Selectors at the FAI held sway and Livingstone left in 1953. He went to Europe and took charge of Belgium, steering them to the 1954 World Cup finals, where his charges are involved in a highly entertaining 4-4 draw with England.

FRIDAY 15TH JANUARY 2010

The FAI announce that Arsenal's Emirates Stadium in north London will be the venue for the 'home' friendly on March 2nd between Ireland and World Cup favourites Brazil.

WEDNESDAY 16TH JANUARY 1980

Today, Millwall's Kevin O'Callaghan – just 18 but already an Ireland under-21 international – is sold to Ipswich after a handful of games. "I am keeping a promise that I made to Kevin," says Millwall manager George Petchey to *The Times*. "I told the boy that if a club came in for him then he could go."

TUESDAY 17TH JANUARY 1979

Jimmy Conway goes west as the Republic of Ireland international leaves Manchester City and signs for Portland Timbers in the North American Soccer League for £10,000. Conway had featured in the Fulham team that reached the 1975 FA Cup Final but played just 13 games for City. A midfielder or winger, and winner of 20 caps for Ireland, he plays three seasons with the Timbers then stays in the country to coach.

THURSDAY 18TH JANUARY 1973

Manchester United manager Tommy Docherty buys Bohemians and Ireland star Mick Martin. He stays at Old Trafford for two seasons before leaving for West Bromwich Albion.

SUNDAY 19TH JANUARY 1969

Steve Staunton, one of Ireland's most capped players and later manager of the national team, is born today. He is briefly with Dundalk but does not make any LOI appearances before he signs for Liverpool in 1986 and spends five seasons with the Anfield club, racking up 65 appearances. He wins his first Irish under-21 cap the next year but is soon promoted to the senior squad, winning the first of what will eventually be 102 caps, in 1988, in a 4-0 win over Tunisia. He plays in one European Championship finals and two World Cup finals and is the first Irishman to play more than 100 times for his country. He leaves Liverpool for Aston Villa but returns to Anfield, only to go back again – via Crystal Palace – to Villa Park. After retiring in 2005, he is surprisingly made Irish manager but his reign is not marked by success.

FRIDAY 20TH JANUARY 1984

The FAI agree Ireland's fixture schedule for the 1986 World Cup qualifiers. Ireland are in group six and will open with a home match against Russia on September 12th, and finish their programme also in Dublin on November 13th when Denmark are the visitors.

SATURDAY 21ST JANUARY 1978

Johnny Giles announces plans to quit as Ireland manager but will not leave for another two years.

SATURDAY 22ND JANUARY 1994

Ireland's recent golden period has put Jack Charlton's side among the group of top seeds in today's draw for the qualifying campaign for Euro 96 in England. The other countries that join Ireland in group six are Portugal, Northern Ireland, Austria, Latvia and Liechtenstein.

TUESDAY 22ND JANUARY 2008

Don Givens tells the FAI that he needs more time to find a replacement for outgoing Irish manager Steve Staunton. Givens is one of the headhunters charged with finding a new manager along with Don Howe and Ray Houghton. Names linked with the job include Gerard Houllier, Terry Venables and Liam Brady. No-one mentions Giovanni Trapattoni.

THURSDAY 23RD JANUARY 1992

Jack Charlton joins an FAI team in Copenhagen to sort out the fixtures for the 1994 World Cup qualifying group with the football associations of Albania, Denmark, Latvia, Lithuania, Northern Ireland and Spain. Ireland are in the only group with seven countries, making negotiations more tricky than usual. Due to rugby union internationals, the FAI cannot use Lansdowne Road at the end of March or October, while the Irish do not want to play in the freezing Baltic during the winter. The eventual programme means that the Irish players will get a break of just four weeks during the summer.

THURSDAY 24TH JANUARY 2008

Gerard Houllier will not be replacing the departed Steve Staunton as Ireland's manager. The former Liverpool boss is happy with his current role at the French Football Federation (FFF), which moves to quell rumours that he may leave. "He has assured the federation that his future is with [us]," FFF spokesman Francois Manardo tells the *Irish Daily Star*. "There has been plenty of speculation linking him with the job as Ireland manager. I can tell you that it is rubbish."

TUESDAY 25TH JANUARY 2000

Willo Flood of Manchester City, and Peterborough United's Rory Hutton, are the only English-based players in an 18-player squad named by Vinnie Butler for the Irish under-15 team's game with Wales on February 3rd.

SUNDAY 26TH JANUARY 1919

Thomas 'Bud' Aherne, a regular at full-back for Ireland, is born. A senior hurler for hometown club Limerick, he also played for Limerick FC before journeying north to play for Belfast Celtic then to England, where he joins Luton Town. Aherne's first Irish cap is against Portugal in Ireland after the war in 1946. He wins 15 more over the next eight years.

SUNDAY 26TH JANUARY 2003

After two defeats in their opening Euro 2004 qualifiers, Mick McCarthy has quit as Ireland manager and today Brian Kerr is confirmed as the FAI's choice as his replacement.

FRIDAY 27TH JANUARY 2006

The FAI are in Montreux in Switzerland for a draw to decide who Ireland will face in the qualifiers for Euro 2008 in Austria and Switzerland. The Irish, who have not appeared in a European finals for eight years, are among the fourth seeds and the draw brings out the Czech Republic, Germany, Slovakia, Wales, Cyprus and San Marino.

THURSDAY 28TH JANUARY 2010

Rob Kiernan, the captain of the Irish under-19 team, joins Kilmarnock on a trial from Watford.

FRIDAY 29TH JANUARY 1988

Owen Garvan, who was born today, has a fine footballing heritage. The grandson of one Irish international, Con Martin, and nephew of another, Mick Martin, Garvan joins Home Farm in 1999 and stays for five years before moving to England and signing for Ipswich Town. He made his debut for the Irish under-21 team in September 2007 against Portugal.

FRIDAY 30TH JANUARY 2009

Ireland will stage its first major European final after the Uefa Executive Committee confirm in Nyon that the FAI has won the right to stage the 2011 Europa League Final at the new Aviva Stadium in Dublin. Due to Uefa's rules against corporate sponsorship, the stadium will be re-titled the Dublin Arena for the duration of the Europa League Final.

REPUBLIC OF IRELAND
On This Day

FEBRUARY

WEDNESDAY 1st FEBRUARY 1961

Johnny Byrne is born in Manchester and has a varied career that takes him from York City to Brighton & Hove Albion (on three separate occasions) and Le Havre in France. Along the way, the striker turns out 23 times for Ireland after making his debut in a 2-1 defeat against Italy in 1985 under the reign of Eoin Hand. He went to Euro 1988, and the 1990 World Cup, as part of Ireland's squad.

TUESDAY 1st FEBRUARY 1977

The birthday of Kevin Kilbane, one of Ireland's most capped players. A left-winger or left-back, he progresses through the ranks at his local side, Preston North End, where he first won Ireland under-21 honours. West Bromwich Albion spend a club-record £1 million on Kilbane in 1997 and he makes his debut for Ireland that same year against Iceland. Jokingly known as 'Zinedine Kilbane' by some Irish fans, he plays in the 2002 World Cup finals and later joins Sunderland, then Everton, and more recently Wigan Athletic and Hull City.

FRIDAY 2nd FEBRUARY 1990

A total of 34 teams have entered qualifying for Euro 92, to be staged in Sweden. In their quest for a place at the eight-team finals, Ireland are today paired with England, Poland and Turkey.

SATURDAY 3rd FEBRUARY 1923

The nascent Irish Free State Football Association (IFSFA) meet a delegation from the Belfast-based Irish Football Association (IFA) in Dublin's Shelbourne Hotel to try and heal the rift between the two bodies. The meeting breaks down after three hours with Captain J. M. Wilton, leader of the IFA party, dismissing the IFSFA's demands as "stupendously impertinent".

WEDNESDAY 4th FEBRUARY 1987

Darren Dea is born in Dublin. A defender, he plays initially for Home Farm before joining Glasgow Celtic, where he wins the first of nine caps for Ireland's under-21 side. In May 2008, he is named in new manager Giovanni Trapattoni's first squad and makes his debut in September the next year against South Africa.

MONDAY 5TH FEBRUARY 1968

The draw for the qualifying campaign for the 1970 World Cup finals in Mexico sees Ireland in a hard section alongside Czechoslovakia, Hungary and Denmark.

TUESDAY 5TH FEBRUARY 1985

Paul McGrath makes his international debut for Ireland in a friendly with Italy in front of 40,000 at Dalymount Park in Dublin. Italy are 2-0 up within 18 minutes and although Gary Waddock reduces the arrears on 53 minutes, the visitors win 2-1.

MONDAY 5TH FEBRUARY 1996

The FAI appoint Mick McCarthy as the new manager of the Republic of Ireland.

WEDNESDAY 6TH FEBRUARY 1980

A crowd of just over 90,000 cram into Wembley as England celebrate coasting through their European Championship qualifying group. Ron Greenwood's team have dropped just one point. That was a 1-1 draw at Lansdowne Road but the Irish need to win at Wembley to beat Northern Ireland to claim second spot behind England. An unfortunate deflection off Ashley Grimes deceives Gerry Peyton to give Kevin Keegan the opening goal on 35 minutes. Peyton then collides with Liverpool's English forward David Johnson and has to be replaced on 62 minutes by Cardiff City's Ron Healey, who is lobbed by Keegan for England's second goal in a 2-0 win.

WEDNESDAY 6TH FEBRUARY 2008

Brazil return to Ireland again, this time to Croke Park, where a crowd of 30,000 see a lacklustre game played in near freezing conditions settled by Robinho's strike on 65 minutes. Robbie Keane has a chance to level in the dying minutes but Julio Cesar reacts quickly to deny the striker.

WEDNESDAY 6TH FEBRUARY 1991

A majestic performance by Ireland today sees Wales thrashed 3-0 in a friendly at the Racecourse. Niall Quinn puts the Irish ahead after 24 minutes and adds another in the second half before John Byrne completes a 3-0 rout four minutes from time.

SATURDAY 7TH FEBRUARY 1959

Mick McCarthy is born in Barnsley, where he starts his footballing career. During his time with the Tykes, the club climbs from the Fourth Division to the Second and he makes more than 270 appearances for the Yorkshire side. Only on leaving in 1983, when he signs for newly relegated Manchester City for £20,000, does he gain international honours. McCarthy is eligible for Ireland because of his Irish father and makes his debut in May 1984 against Poland. He goes on to win 57 caps, playing in Euro 88, where he is Ireland's captain, and the 1990 World Cup finals. After retiring, he moves into club management with Millwall in 1992 and four years later takes over as Ireland's boss, leading the team to the 2002 World Cup finals after which he leaves and returns to the club game.

FRIDAY 7TH FEBRUARY 1986

The 19 members of the FAI's executive council gather on the ground floor of its headquarters at 80 Merrion Street to finally decide who will be Ireland's next manager. One committee member, Tony O'Neill, asks for a postponement to allow the FAI to talk to Brian Clough, who has expressed interest in trying to combine the job on a part-time basis with his club post at Nottingham Forest. The meeting will not be postponed but FAI president Des Casey has also spoken to Bob Paisley, whose name is added to a ballot now also including Johnny Giles, Liam Tuohy and Jack Charlton. After a number of ballots, Charlton beats Paisley by ten votes to eight.

WEDNESDAY 7TH FEBRUARY 2007

The tiny Olimpico Stadium in San Marino is rammed with 3,294 supporters, mostly from Ireland, as Steve Staunton's side are the visitors for today's European Championship qualifier. Many leave wishing they had not bothered. The game is goalless at half-time. Kevin Kilbane gives Ireland the lead soon after the break but San Marino, who will manage just two goals in a dozen Euro 2008 qualifiers, score one today, Manuel Marani levelling a minute before time to the derision of many Irish fans. In the last kick of the game, Stephen Ireland rescues his team from what could be their worst-ever result ever. Even a 2-1 win is not far off.

CAST OF *I, KEANO*, A SHOW ABOUT THE SPECTACULAR FALL-OUT BETWEEN ROY KEANE AND MICK McCARTHY, OPENED ON FEBRUARY 8TH 2005.

SUNDAY 7TH FEBRUARY 2010

Ireland are placed with Russia, Slovakia, Macedonia, Armenia and Andorra in the qualifiers for Euro 2012, to be held jointly in Poland and the Ukraine.

TUESDAY 7TH FEBRUARY 1989

Jack Charlton and Michel Platini are in their respective dug-outs as Ireland and France grind out a 0-0 draw in a friendly international watched by 22,000 at Dalymount Park.

TUESDAY 8TH FEBRUARY 2005

I, Keano, a musical about the row between Roy Keane and Mick McCarthy in Saipan during the 2002 World Cup, opens at the Olympia Theatre in Dublin. A host of celebrities, including sports presenter Bill O'Herlihy, comedian Pat Shortt, Boyzone star Keith Duffy and members of the Irish rugby union team, attend the premiere. Written by Arthur Mathews, Michael Nugent, Paul Woodfull and Conor Phillips, the story is presented as a mock-epic melodrama about an ancient Roman legion preparing for war and generates an estimated €10 million in ticket sales over the next two years. "This is a play that captures perfectly the passion, posturing and lunacy of the time when the country was convulsed by the confrontation between Roy Keane – the combative Manchester United skipper who almost provoked a sporting civil war in his native Ireland when he walked out on its World Cup squad in 2002 – and the then Irish manager Mick McCarthy," writes theatre newspaper *The Stage*.

MONDAY 9TH FEBRUARY 1987

The birthday of Joseph O'Cearuill, who was born in Edmonton, north London, but opts to play for Ireland. With Arsenal as a junior, he makes his Ireland debut in 2007 but leaves Highbury, initially for Brighton & Hove Albion, then Barnet, before spending time in the LOI with St Patrick's Athletic.

THURSDAY 10TH FEBRUARY 1994

Two days after undergoing a worrying brain scan, Jack Charlton announces to the media today that he is fine in typical fashion: "They had, indeed, located a brain," he says. "And yes, it seems to be in reasonably good working order."

WEDNESDAY 10TH FEBRUARY 1999

Mick McCarthy's team need a penalty from Denis Irwin on 38 minutes to break down a stubborn Paraguayan defence in a friendly at Lansdowne Road. A second-half strike from David Connolly gives Ireland a 2-0 win.

TUESDAY 11TH FEBRUARY 1986

Jack Charlton arrives in Dublin to take up his new job as manager of Ireland.

TUESDAY 11TH FEBRUARY 1997

A superb performance in the Welsh goal from Mark Crossley denies a resurgent Republic of Ireland side in a friendly at a rain-swept Arms Park, where a crowd of just 7,000 witness Paul McGrath's 83rd and final appearance in Irish colours. In a match played in near monsoon conditions, Bobby Gould's team get few chances against an Irish defence well marshalled by 37-year-old McGrath, Ireland's most-capped player who has returned after a period out of the side. Apart from McGrath, the Irish side are mostly youngsters, such as debutant Ian Harte, but still manage to dominate Wales. "We did enough to win comfortably, but their goalkeeper was inspired," says Irish skipper Steve Staunton. "I cruised through the game relatively unfussed," recalled McGrath in his autobiography *Back from the Brink*, but he never plays for Ireland again.

WEDNESDAY 11TH FEBRUARY 1998

Ireland rarely play B internationals and today's 1-0 defeat at home in Dublin to Northern Ireland is only the eighth staged since 1957.

SUNDAY 12TH FEBRUARY 1928

Ireland's first international win comes today. Since making their official international debut in 1926, Ireland are managing a game a season and this year's fixture takes Ireland to Liege and a fixture with Belgium, the 1920 Olympic champions. Belgium are two goals up at half-time, when a terrible thunderstorm turns into sleet and the boggy pitch changes the nature of the game. Ireland revive sensationally in the last 45 minutes. Jimmy White of Bohemians gets a brace, Billy Lacy of Shelbourne another and a penalty on 79 minutes rammed home by Jack Sullivan of Fordsons seals a sensational 4-2 success.

WEDNESDAY 12TH FEBRUARY 2003

Two goals in the first 16 minutes from Kevin Kilbane and Clinton Morrison give Ireland a 2-0 win over Scotland at Hampden Park in a friendly.

FRIDAY 13TH FEBRUARY 1956

Liam Brady, probably one of the most talented players ever produced by Ireland, is born today in Dublin. At the age of 15, he moves to London, joins Arsenal and makes his debut in October 1973 against Birmingham City. By the 1974/75 season, Brady is a regular and stars in the club's 1979 FA Cup victory. He is made PFA Footballer of the Year and wins the European Cup Winners' Cup before Juventus sign Brady for £514,000. He spends seven years in Italy playing later for Sampdoria, Inter Milan and Ascoli before finishing his career back in England with West Ham United, then retiring in 1990. His elder brother Ray played professionally in England for Millwall and Queens Park Rangers and made half a dozen appearances for Ireland but after making his debut in 1974 against the Soviet Union, Liam goes on to win 72 caps over the next 16 years with Ireland. In 1991, he moves into management and takes over at Glasgow Celtic, leaving after two years and then managing Brighton & Hove Albion for two seasons. He works as a pundit for RTÉ before returning to Highbury to work with the youth teams, a job he combined for two seasons with one as Ireland's assistant manager.

WEDNESDAY 13TH FEBRUARY 2002

A crowd of 44,000 swell Lansdowne Road as Ireland play their first match since securing qualification for this year's World Cup finals. Mick McCarthy's team overcome Russia 2-0 in a friendly with goals from Steven Reid and Robbie Keane.

WEDNESDAY 13TH FEBRUARY 2008

Giovanni Trapattoni is at last officially unveiled as Ireland's new manager. A seven-time winner of Serie A, the 68-year-old Italian's appointment comes 113 days after Steve Staunton's reign ended. "Ireland are not a second-rate team, they are supposed to be a first-rate team," Trapattoni, who previously managed Italy from 2000 to 2004, tells *The Times*.

SUNDAY 14TH FEBRUARY 1965

After months of disputes between the FAI, the LOI, and officials in Syria over a suitable date, today was set aside for Ireland to entertain Syria in a vital World Cup qualifier – only for the Middle Eastern side to pull out. The withdrawal was much to the chagrin of FAI secretary Joe Wickham, who worked tirelessly to try and find a date to suit everyone for this first leg and the return, which had been scheduled for Damascus on May 15th. Syria's withdrawal gave Ireland a bye through to the next round, where Spain would be their opponents.

MONDAY 15TH FEBRUARY 2010

The latest Umbro international kit for Ireland is unveiled at Carroll's FAI Store on Westmoreland Street in Dublin. The kit is a darker shade of St Patrick's green with a new version of the FAI crest trimmed in gold, gold seam detail and a new design. "The overall look takes inspiration from vintage Irish kits and pays homage to the past in terms of the heritage of Irish teams and an understanding of what it means to be Irish," says Lorcan O'Connor, a director of Carroll's FAI store.

WEDNESDAY 15TH FEBRUARY 1995

A black day for football generally, and England's travelling fans in particular, after a riot at Lansdowne Road. David Kelly's strike on 23 minutes puts Ireland 1-0 up but a minority of England fans tear seats from the stands and throw them onto the pitch. After 27 minutes Dutch referee Dick Jol abandons the game and Jack Charlton and Terry Venables lead their players from the field. More than 70 people are injured – mostly English – and the Irish Army has to escort the visiting fans away from Lansdowne Road. The two sides have not met since but the FAI have indicated an interest in England playing at the new Aviva Stadium.

FRIDAY 16TH FEBRUARY 1996

Sean Connolly resigns as the FAI's chief executive shortly after Michael Morris quit as the association's accountant. Days later, Joe McGrath, the FAI's national director of coaching, departs to take on a similar role in New Zealand, as a storm gathers at the FAI.

TUESDAY 17th FEBRUARY 1987

Ireland's under-21 team are thrashed 4-1 by Scotland in a European qualifier in Edinburgh.

WEDNESDAY 17th FEBRUARY 1993

Ireland play Wales at Tolka Park and Tommy Coyne scores nine minutes from time to give the hosts a 2-1 win. Mark Hughes had opened the scoring after a quarter of an hour and Wales had led until Kevin Sheedy restored parity on 75 minutes.

FRIDAY 17th FEBRUARY 2006

Despite losing 15 of their original squad through withdrawals, Ireland win the Madeira under-21 tournament for the second time in three years by beating Portugal 2-1. Earlier, Ireland had drawn with hosts Madeira 1-1 and beaten Finland 2-1. Today, goals from Stephen Grant of Waterford United and 17-year-old Anthony Ward of Bohemians give Ireland a win against a Portuguese side that only needed a draw to claim the trophy.

WEDNESDAY 18th FEBRUARY 1987

After draws in their first two European Championship qualifiers, Ireland register their first win in the competition under Jack Charlton as a Mark Lawrenson goal on eight minutes is enough to settle the match with Scotland in front of a 45,000 crowd at Hampden Park.

WEDNESDAY 18th FEBRUARY 2004

The FAI paid out a reported £500,000 to bring Brazil to Lansdowne Road. Tickets sell out within 15 minutes. Brian Kerr's team are not overawed by the quintuple World Cup winners. Stephen Carr and Robbie Keane both have chances to score for Ireland either side of half-time. Shay Given and the woodwork save Ireland, who also have chances. A fine Andy O'Brien challenge at the end keeps the game goalless but Ireland deserve a 0-0 draw.

WEDNESDAY 19th FEBRUARY 1992

Wales get their revenge for a 3-0 thrashing in Wrexham last year as Ireland put in a sterile performance at the Royal Society Showground in Dublin. A Mark Pembridge goal on 72 minutes seals a 1-0 win.

TUESDAY 20TH FEBRUARY 1967

Born today, Mike Milligan was sold for millions of pounds during his career but featured just once for Ireland. After five years with Oldham Athletic, he joined Everton but soon returned to Boundary Park for another three seasons, totalling more than 270 appearances in his two spells. During his second period at Oldham, he won his only Irish cap coming on as a 61st-minute substitute for Denis Irwin in a 4-1 win over the US.

THURSDAY 21ST FEBRUARY 2008

Reading striker Kevin Doyle reveals that all of his Ireland teammates are desperate to impress new manager Giovanni Trapattoni. "His appointment is good news. He's been very successful," Doyle tells today's *Evening Herald*.

WEDNESDAY 22ND FEBRUARY 1967

Ireland's hopes of further progress in the European Championships virtually end in Ankara. A scattering of snow fell in Turkey before the game that sees both teams start tentatively before Ayhan Elmastasoglu dribbles through Ireland's defence after 35 minutes to score. Ireland have a shot cleared off the line but Ogun Altiparmak doubles Turkey's lead on 78 minutes. Alan Kelly makes two fine saves before Noel Cantwell grabs a last-minute consolation for Ireland, who must now beat Czechoslovakia home and away to stand any chance of qualifying.

WEDNESDAY 23RD FEBRUARY 2000

The summer's European Championship finals will not involve Ireland and today's friendly with the Czech Republic – runners-up at the last Euro finals – is the start of Mick McCarthy's preparations for the 2002 World Cup qualifiers with Sunderland's Paul Butler making his debut. The giant Czech striker Jan Koller scores after just four minutes at Lansdowne Road but Ireland win an entertaining tie 3-2 through an own goal, an Ian Harte strike, and a last-minute effort from Robbie Keane.

FRIDAY 24TH FEBRUARY 1978

The squad for Ireland's first-ever under-21 international is named today. Players called up include Ashley Grimes of Manchester United and Terry Grealish of Leyton Orient. The fixture against Northern Ireland in Dublin finishes 1-1.

TUESDAY 24TH FEBRUARY 1981

Eamon O'Keefe wins his first full cap for Ireland, who lose 3-1 at home to Wales at Tolka Park. O'Keefe wins four more caps in an irregular international career that ends in 1985. He holds the record as the oldest player to win an under-21 cap after playing against China aged 30. "I played as an over-aged player for Ireland against China a few times, and scored a couple of goals," O'Keefe tells *The Guardian* in 2010. "I only scored against them, though, and people thought I'd had a dodgy Chinese takeaway or something such was my willingness to score!"

SATURDAY 24TH FEBRUARY 1996

Merriongate: at an FAI senior council meeting in Dublin, it is revealed that honorary treasurer Joe Delaney personally met the shortfall of a reported £110,000 from ticket sales during the 1994 World Cup finals. Within days, President Louis Kilcoyne is asked to quit. An FAI meeting on March 8th sees a swathe of resignations, including Delaney, who cites an error of judgement.

SUNDAY 25TH FEBRUARY 1934

Ireland make their World Cup debut against Belgium at Dalymount Park. On his debut, Peadar Gaskins is captain. Ireland have faced Belgium four times in their last nine games and never lost but come close today in a thrilling tie that is memorable for Paddy Moore's contribution. The Aberdeen player levels the scores on 27 minutes. Minutes into the second half, Belgium are 3-1 up but Moore keeps on pegging the Belgians back. His strike 15 minutes from time takes his haul to four as the fixture finishes 4-4. The game is the highest-scoring international draw Ireland have been involved in.

SATURDAY 26TH FEBRUARY 2005

John Delaney will take over next month as the new full-time chief executive of the FAI. The son of former treasurer Joe Delaney, he had been doing the job on a temporary basis since the end of last year.

FRIDAY 27TH FEBRUARY 1981

The birthday of Irish international Yvonne Tracey, who began her career with Lifford. She joins England's premier ladies team Arsenal in 2000 and has won more than 40 caps for Ireland. In 2002 she was voted Irish international Player of the Year.

WEDNESDAY 27TH FEBRUARY 1985

A crowd of just 3,000 are scattered around the Ramat-Gan stadium in Tel-Aviv despite the ground playing host to a double header. Israel's under-21 team go down 2-1 to England before Israel's senior side take on Ireland in a friendly international. The crowd is boosted by a contingent of Irish United Nations troops given a day off to see if Eoin Hand's team can avenge last year's 3-0 thrashing by Israel. The closest either side comes to a goal is a Gary Waddock shot that bounces back off the bar on 54 minutes.

FRIDAY 27TH FEBRUARY 2004

Don Givens' Irish under-21 team beat Madeira 4-0 to win a tournament on the Portuguese island after drawing with Portugal 0-0 and beating Italy 1-0 in their previous matches.

SUNDAY 28TH FEBRUARY 1932

Noel Euchuria Cantwell is born today and is brought up near the Mardyke, the centre of sport in Cork. A talented footballer and cricketer, he would go on to represent Ireland in both sports. He begins his football career with Western Rovers and is often in the shadow of older brother Frank, but Noel wins a contract with West Ham United in 1952. He spends eight years with the club, making more than 240 appearances and breaking into the Ireland team in 1953. Cantwell is a full-back but he would score 14 goals in 36 appearances for Ireland. He signed for Manchester United in 1960 and won two First Division titles, later turning to management after retiring in 1967. His first job was to replace Jimmy Hill at Coventry City and the Sky Blues qualified for the Uefa Cup under Cantwell. He later managed both Peterborough United and the New England Tea Men on two occasions. Noel Cantwell died on September 8th 2005, aged 73.

FRIDAY 29TH FEBRUARY 1983

Captain Robbie Creevy and regular defender Gary Murphy are missing for Ireland's schoolboys, who go a goal down after just nine minutes to Wales at St Helen's in Swansea. John Mulroy equalises in the second half and substitute Kevin Barry seals a 2-1 win for Ireland ten minutes from time.

REPUBLIC OF IRELAND
On This Day

MARCH

MONDAY 1st MARCH 1926

Ireland's selectors name the team that will play in their country's first fully recognised international. The matches at the 1924 Olympics are not recognised by Fifa but returning from Amsterdam the IFSFA contacted Italy about a game. Setting a date proved a lengthy experience but today the selectors name the squad to travel to Turin for the game on May 26th: Bohemians – Harry Cannon and Jack McCarthy; Shamrock Rovers – Dinny Doyle, John Joe Flood, Bob Fullam and Jack Fagan; Shelbourne – Mick Foley, captain; Fordstons – Frank Brady and James Connolly; Drumcondra – Joe Grace; Athlone Town – Ned Brooks. Three reserves are named and J. L. Brennan, chairman of the Free State Council, will also travel to run the line.

TUESDAY 2nd MARCH 1971

The birthday of Damien Duff, who hails from Ballyboden. He plays for Leicester Celtic, Lourdes Celtic and St. Kevin's Boys as a youth but signs for Blackburn Rovers in 1996 as a trainee. Duff makes his debut on the last day of the 1996/97 season against Leicester City and wins his first cap for Ireland in 1988 against the Czech Republic. Before this, Duff played in the 1997 and 1999 World Youth Cups and in the first tournament in Malaysia scored a golden goal – the first scored in the tournament by an Irish player. A winger, he is one of Ireland's most capped players.

TUESDAY 2nd MARCH 2010

"Nah, he was just telling me about his good mate Jesus and all that," Keith Andrews tells the media, denying an argument with Kaka during Ireland's game against Brazil at the Emirates Stadium in north London. The fixture is played in front of a 40,000 crowd but not one to remember for the Blackburn Rovers midfielder, who puts a marvellous Robinho cross into his own net at the end of the first half. The mercurial Brazilian, whose time at Manchester City this season has proved so very disappointing, then scores himself on 77 minutes. Grafite back-heels a pass through the legs of Hull City's Paul McShane, leaving Robinho to simply side-foot the ball into the net for a 2-0 win.

TUESDAY 3RD MARCH 1953

Brian Kerr, the only man to win two international tournaments with Irish national teams, is born. A boxer as a young man, he also played football for Shelbourne but realised he would not have much of a career as a player so began coaching, initially with Crumlin United under-11s. His first senior job was at Shamrock Rovers and then in December 1986 he is appointed coach of St Patrick's. Three weeks later he wins the Leinster Senior Cup – the club's first trophy in a decade. In 1990, St. Pats win the LOI title. Six years later, he takes over as technical director for the FAI youth sides from ages 16 to 20. The under-20s qualified for the World Cup for the first time in 1997, and the under-16s and under-18s win their respective European titles. His career as Ireland's senior coach was less successful, lasting just two years.

SUNDAY 4TH MARCH 1990

Patrick 'Paddy' Madden is born in Coolock, Dublin. A striker with Bohemians, Madden was a member of the Ireland under-19s team then makes his debut for the Irish under-21 side the following year.

FRIDAY 5TH MARCH 1971

Ireland's amateur side lose 1-0 to England in Dublin.

THURSDAY 6TH MARCH 2008

Liam Brady will be able to take time out of his youth team job at Arsenal to help Giovanni Trapattoni as he starts his new job as Ireland manager. "The board of directors and [manager] Arsene Wenger are quite happy for me to do this and to keep my job at Arsenal," Brady told RTÉ.

SUNDAY 7TH MARCH 1954

The first away victory in the World Cup for Ireland, who travel to Luxembourg and record a 1-0 win over the Grand Duchy in a qualifier. Already out, Ireland field a number of reserves against the whipping boys of Europe but the tactic nearly backfires. Civil servant Roger Weydert twice nearly puts Luxembourg in front in the first half, while Karrier hits an upright. Ireland improve after the break and George Cummins strikes the winner on 62 minutes.

WEDNESDAY 8TH MARCH 1950

Tom Aherne, Con Martin, Reg Ryan and Dave Walsh become the first players to turn out for two national teams in the same World Cup tournament when the quartet of internationals from the Republic play for Northern Ireland in a World Cup qualifier with Wales. After the match, Joe Cunningham, chairman of Shamrock Rovers, writes to all four of the English-based players asking them never to play for Northern Ireland again. The issue went all the way to Fifa, who side with the FAI. Players only represent one team soon after.

SATURDAY 8TH MARCH 1952

Ireland's amateur team travel to Shrewsbury in England for their first away game with their English counterparts but go down 8-3. The match is only the second-ever fixture between the two countries' amateur teams and the win extends England's unbeaten record to 15 matches.

FRIDAY 8TH MARCH 1968

Ireland's amateur XI slump to a 6-0 defeat in a friendly with the Great Britain Olympic team. On the bench for the hosts in Watford is future Manchester United star Alan Gowling, then still on amateur forms at Old Trafford.

WEDNESDAY 8TH MARCH 1989

Despite regular fixtures during the early years of Irish football before World War II, Ireland have not faced Hungary for two decades before today's World Cup qualifier at the Nepstadion in Budapest. Half a dozen Hungarian players have recently been banned for match-fixing. The manager also recently quit but the Hungarians are still Ireland's closest qualifying rivals behind favourites Spain. Hungary have skills, Ireland grit, and the visitors come off feeling "disappointed" with a 0-0 draw according to John Aldridge.

SATURDAY 9TH MARCH 1974

Irish youth international John Waters is only third choice for a midfield slot at his club Leicester City but comes into the national team after a spate of injuries and marks his first XI debut by scoring both goals in the Foxes' league win at Queens Park Rangers.

SUNDAY 10TH MARCH 1968

Donogh O'Malley, Fianna Fáil politician and president of the FAI, dies suddenly while out campaigning at a by-election in County Clare. He had been FAI president since 1965 and is just 47. He is buried with a full state funeral.

WEDNESDAY 11TH MARCH 1964

Four decades earlier, Ireland reached the quarter-finals of the Olympics, today they take on Spain in the quarter-finals of the Nations Cup… but the game is not one to remember. In a match dubbed the 'Slaughter of Seville' by *World Soccer*, Ireland are totally undone by the hosts in a blistering start to the tie. Varela opens the scoring after five minutes and Blanch adds another seven minutes later. Matt McEvoy pulls a goal back on 18 minutes but Varela and Cao ensure that Spain go in at half-time 4-1 up with the two-legged tie virtually won. Ireland put on a better showing in the second half but a minute from time, Cao wraps up a 5-1 win in front of 27,200 fans.

THURSDAY 12TH MARCH 1931

George Cummins, inside-forward for Everton, Luton Town and Ireland, is born in Dublin. He plays for St Patrick's Athletic before joining Everton in 1951, and makes his debut for Ireland two years later, scoring five goals in 19 matches over the next eight years. He played in the 1959 FA Cup Final with Luton and died in November 2009, aged 78.

SUNDAY 13TH MARCH 1960

Ireland's amateur side try to get their campaign to qualify for the football tournament at this summer's Olympic Games in Rome back on track with a victory over Britain. The visitors squeaked home 3-2 in last year's first leg in Brighton, when they were without former Chelsea striker Jim Lewis, now back in the amateur game with Walthamstow Avenue. Lewis is back in the British XI in Dublin and the visitors cruise home 3-1, ending Irish dreams of another appearance in the Olympic Games. The game is the last competitive football fixture between the Republic of Ireland and a team representing the whole of the United Kingdom of Great Britain and Northern Ireland.

FRIDAY 14TH MARCH 1980

Colin Healy is born in Cork. A midfielder, his career takes him from Glasgow Celtic to Sunderland, Livingston and Barnsley. In the 2002/03 season, he breaks into the Ireland side, winning a dozen caps but not playing again. In 2007, Healy and former international Gareth Farrelly were briefly suspended by Fifa, when they tried to sign for Cork City. Fifa ruled that the duo had contravened a rule banning players from signing for more than one club in 12 months.

FRIDAY 15TH MARCH 1946

The birthday of John Dempsey, who is born in Hampstead, north London. A centre-back with Fulham, Chelsea and Ireland, he wins 19 caps in a five-year career that starts in 1966. He won the FA Cup and Cup Winners' Cup during a nine-year career with Chelsea. After a spell at their neighbours Fulham, he finishes his career with the Philadelphia Fury in the US. He briefly manages Dundalk in the early 1980s but only lasts six months in the job before leaving by mutual consent.

MONDAY 16TH MARCH 1981

The FAI accept – for the time being – a ban on Eamon O'Keefe and the Everton player is excluded from the squad named for next week's World Cup qualifier with Belgium. O'Keefe played for Ireland in a 3-1 defeat against Wales last month but appeared for England in a semi-professional tournament in 1979 and Fifa rule he must not play for the Irish again. "We have accepted Fifa's decision for the time being," FAI president Brendon Menton tells *The Times*. "But we intend to pursue the matter. We feel that there are certain facts which indicate that O'Keefe will be able to play for the Republic again." O'Keefe goes on to make four more appearances for Ireland.

TUESDAY 17TH MARCH 1936

The IFSFA play as Ireland for the first time, taking on the Swiss and William Glen's team avenge a 1-0 defeat in the only other meeting between the two sides a year ago in Basel. Arsenal's Jimmy Dunne taps in the only goal of the game to beat the 1934 World Cup quarter-finalists in front of a 32,000 crowd at Dalymount Park.

IRISH MANAGER GIOVANNI TRAPATONNI WAS BORN ON ST PATRICK'S DAY IN 1939.

SATURDAY 17TH MARCH 1945

Irish international full-back Paddy Mulligan is born. Gary Waddock is another international also born on St Patrick's Day (in 1962), while the team's Italian manager Giovanni Trapattoni celebrates his birthday today. He was born in 1939.

WEDNESDAY 18TH MARCH 2009

The FAI sign a new ten-year €25.6 million contract with Umbro that ties Ireland to the kit maker until 2020.

THURSDAY 18TH MARCH 2010

Former Cork City, Drogheda and University College Dublin boss Paul Doolin is named manager of Ireland's under-23 team.

SUNDAY 19TH MARCH 1939

Hungary, runners-up in last year's World Cup, are the visitors for the first international played outside Dublin. The Mardyke, then home to Cork City, is the venue. The Irish had won their last two fixtures and were not overawed, scoring after just 14 minutes. Paddy Bradshaw had scored in each of his last four games for St. James's Gate and continues that record today but a last-minute goal from Johnny Carey is needed to rescue a draw. The Mardyke was full to its 18,000 capacity but Cork would not host another international for 46 years.

TUESDAY 20TH MARCH 1923

Cornelius 'Con' Martin is born in Rush, Dublin. A fine technical player, he plays for Drumcondra and Glentoran then spends the next nine years with Leeds United and Aston Villa. Martin was selected, along with Reg Ryan, Tommy Aherne and Davy Walsh, for Northern Ireland in a British Championship match in 1950 – the last time players from the south played for Northern Ireland. He was asked to pull out three days before the game but refuses to do so. "Jackie Vernon had pulled out of the team with an injury and I was chosen to captain the team," Martin is quoted as saying in *Football Association of Ireland 75 Years*. "Now, here was I being put in a position in which I, too, would withdraw at the 11th hour and I wasn't prepared to do that."

FRIDAY 21st MARCH 2010

Not so long ago, Steve Staunton was involved in European Championship qualifiers as manager of Ireland. Today he is sacked as boss of the Football League's bottom club after Darlington sink to a 2-1 home defeat against Barnet watched by just 1,463 people. "It is with regret that we're having to part company with another manager during what's been a forgettable season for us, but we felt we were left with no alternative after yesterday," says chairman Raj Singh. "We desperately wanted things to work out for Steve but it clearly wasn't to be and we will have to take stock again." Darlington finish the season bottom and sink out of the Football League and into the Blue Square Premier League.

TUESDAY 22nd MARCH 1983

Gerry Daly has been a stalwart of the Irish side for virtually the past decade but he is left out of the squad named today for the forthcoming European Championship qualifier in Malta.

MONDAY 23rd MARCH 1953

Just two days before Ireland are due to play Austria in Dublin, Luton Town left-back Tommy Aherne has to pull out of the team due to injury.

WEDNESDAY 23rd MARCH 1988

David Kelly's last-minute effort is the 200th scored by Ireland in internationals played at home as Jack Charlton's team beat Romania 2-0 in a friendly watched by a 30,000 crowd at Lansdowne Road. Kevin Moran scores the other goal on 30 minutes.

WEDNESDAY 24th MARCH 1965

The 100th international for Ireland, who take on Belgium – a regular opponent in the Irish team's early days – today at Dalymount Park but there is nothing to celebrate, the visitors winning 2-0.

WEDNESDAY 24th MARCH 1976

Goals from Liam Brady, Jim Holmes and Mike Walsh see Ireland to a comfortable 3-0 win over Norway in a friendly watched by 22,000 fans at Dalymount Park.

SATURDAY 24TH MARCH 2001

When Mick McCarthy flew out of Dublin for today's World Cup qualifier in Nicosia against Cyprus, he knew that he had seen his father, who is dying of cancer, for the last time. Sadly, two days before the game he passes away. That same day, Cypriot coach Stavros Papadopoulos faxes his condolences to the Irish team's hotel, where McCarthy has to take difficult decisions. Alan Kelly – now third-choice at Blackburn – is dropped in favour of Shay Given, and Richard Dunne keeps his place at centre-half despite Kenny Cunningham, the player he replaced, returning from injury. On the field, Cyprus are routed with Roy Keane and Ian Harte scoring in the first half, then Gary Kelly adding a third before Keane finishes off a 4-0 win by scoring his second two minutes from time. The result was better than the performance but after the game Papadopoulos says that Ireland are quite capable of beating Portugal to top spot in the qualifying group.

SATURDAY 24TH MARCH 2007

History is made as Croke Park, the spiritual home of Ireland's Gaelic football community, stages a football match for the first time. A crowd of 67,000 swells the ground and Stephen Ireland bags all three points for Ireland with a goal in the 39th minute for a 1-0 win over Wales.

WEDNESDAY 24TH MARCH 2010

After nearly a decade in the role, Don Givens steps down as the manager of Ireland's under-21 team. "I have enjoyed the job for ten years now and would like to thank all of the people who assisted me in the role over that time," said Givens, who will stay with the FAI in a scouting capacity.

WEDNESDAY 25TH MARCH 1953

A crowd of 40,000 gather at Dalymount Park to watch Ireland play Austria in Jackie Carey's last international. Goalless at half-time, Ireland are driven on by Captain Carey for the last time and produce a bravura second half to crush the Austrians 4-0 with Alf Ringstead getting a brace and Tommy Eglington and Frank O'Farrell the others. Carey finishes with 29 caps for Ireland and three goals.

WEDNESDAY 25TH MARCH 1981

Mark Lawrenson is injured then David O'Leary fails a fitness test shortly before kick-off in today's World Cup qualifier with Belgium in Brussels. On a storm-sodden pitch, Ireland take the lead only for the Portuguese referee to disallow Frank Stapleton's strike. Jan Ceulemans nets the winner three minutes from time. Eoin Hand confronts Raul Navare after the match before Micky Walsh, then with Porto and with passable Portuguese, makes his own contribution too.

WEDNESDAY 25TH MARCH 1992

John Aldridge becomes the first substitute to come on and score a penalty for Ireland, when he seals a 2-1 win over Switzerland in a friendly at Lansdowne Road today. Alain Sutter had put the visitors ahead after 26 minutes. Tommy Coyne equalised minutes later and the match looked to be heading for a draw until Aldridge's introduction and his spot kick two minutes from time.

WEDNESDAY 25TH MARCH 2009

After much discussion, the football associations of the Republic of Ireland, Wales, Northern Ireland and Scotland meet in the Danish capital of Copenhagen to agree a provisional schedule for a revived Home Nations championship. The tournament will run on a home and away league basis with the first pair of matches on February 8th and 9th 2011 and the remaining fixtures on May 24th and 28th. "After many months of work we are delighted that this has now come about," says Football Association of Wales secretary general David Collins. "We look forward to a great tournament, especially in the new stadium in Dublin, and we trust it will be a huge success."

THURSDAY 25TH MARCH 2010

The FAI agree a fixture list for the Euro 2012 qualifiers that will see a visit to Armenia on September 3rd, followed by the first competitive match at the new Aviva Stadium four days later, when Andorra will be the visitors. "On balance, these fixtures are better than those we had in the previous World Cup qualification campaign," Ireland manager Giovanni Trapattoni tells RTÉ. "I also think the squad will have benefited from the significant steps forward made against top sides like Bulgaria, Montenegro, Italy, France and Brazil."

SUNDAY 26TH MARCH 1926

The official debut of Ireland in international football involves a trip to Turin and a game with Italy, who have played 21 internationals since 1921. Most of the Italians had 10 or more caps and the Irish side had a sharp introduction to international football. Adolfo Baloncieri of Turin scored after just 13 minutes, Mario Magnozzi of Livorno added a second on 36 minutes and Fulvio Bernadini of Lazio a third just before half-time. Ireland stem the Italian tide in the second half but are still sunk 3-0.

WEDNESDAY 26TH MARCH 1980

For the first time, two teams will qualify from Ireland's World Cup qualifying group but the Irish had a low seeding and ended up with a poor draw, facing Belgium, France and the Dutch. Victory over Cyprus in their opening qualifier today is essential. Cyprus had one win in 23 World Cup qualifiers – against Northern Ireland in 1962 – but Johnny Giles' team make hard work of the game at the Makarios Stadium in Nicosia. Paul McGee opens the scoring on eight minutes and Ireland are confidently leading 3-1 after two Mark Lawrenson goals before David O'Leary trips Sotiris Laifas on 74 minutes. Laifas scores the resulting penalty, setting up an unnecessarily nervy last quarter – but Ireland win 3-2. Three weeks later, Giles quits as manager after seven years.

TUESDAY 26TH MARCH 1985

Liam Brady wins his 50th cap for Ireland and marks the occasion by scoring after Gary Bailey fumbles his shot from Frank Stapleton's cross at Wembley but England win 2-1.

WEDNESDAY 26TH MARCH 1986

An Ian Rush goal after just 16 minutes consigns Ireland to a 1-0 friendly defeat against Wales in front of 16,500 at Lansdowne Road.

SATURDAY 26TH MARCH 2005

Clinton Morrison puts Ireland into the lead four minutes into today's qualifier in Tel Aviv, where a 41,000 crowd at the Ramat-Gan Stadium boo Ireland in the warm-ups. Israel, under Avram Grant, fight back. Home keeper Dudu Awat barely has a save to make after Clinton's opener. At the death, Abbas Souan grabs a goal and a point for the hosts. "We have dropped two big points," admits Shay Given to *The Guardian*.

WEDNESDAY 27TH MARCH 1991

Ireland's last match at Wembley before the old stadium is knocked down sees England subjected to an aerial bombardment. The hosts take an undeserved lead after just nine minutes when Steve Staunton's defensive header drops to Lee Dixon, whose shot is deflected past Packie Bonner. Less than twenty minutes later Niall Quinn converts a Paul McGrath centre and Ireland should have taken all the points in this European Championship qualifier, but Graham Taylor's men hang on for a draw.

WEDNESDAY 28TH MARCH 1990

Bernie Slaven makes his debut and scores four minutes from time to claim a 1-0 win for Ireland over Wales in a friendly at Lansdowne Road in front of a 41,350 crowd. Three months later, Slaven is at the World Cup finals in Italy as part of Ireland's squad but does not get a game.

WEDNESDAY 28TH MARCH 2001

The Irish squad flew directly from their last World Cup qualifier in Cyprus to Barcelona for tonight's game with Andorra but Mick McCarthy, who has just lost his father to cancer, returns home in between. The build-up to the game is overshadowed by the arrival of an anonymous fax at Fifa's headquarters in Switzerland claiming half the Andorran side are ineligible. Midfielder Marc Bernaus will face Damien Duff again having played against the Irishman in the 1997 World Youth Cup finals in Malaysia for Spain. A pompous Fifa official asks both teams to identify themselves, even Roy Keane. Andorra play in Barcelona if a home game is going to involve a decent level of away support, such as the 5,000 Irish fans present, but despite ceding home advantage the game is scoreless until an Ian Harte penalty settles Irish nerves on 33 minutes. Two late goals from Kevin Kilbane and Matt Holland make the scoreline more respectable for Ireland.

WEDNESDAY 28TH MARCH 2007

Shay Given becomes only the second goalkeeper – after Alan Kelly – to captain Ireland. Given takes the armband for a European Championship qualifier and keeps a clean sheet as Kevin Doyle's goal after 13 minutes is enough for victory over Slovakia.

SATURDAY 28TH MARCH 2009

Ireland miss a hatful of chances and drop a point at home in a 0-0 draw with Bulgaria in a World Cup qualifier. "We never make things easy for ourselves," remarks captain Robbie Keane to *The Guardian.* "We have to pick ourselves up now and look forward to Wednesday." That game is against Italy in Bari.

TUESDAY 29TH MARCH 1983

The FAI sends a letter of complaint to Uefa over the state of the pitch at Malta's National Stadium in Ta'Qali for tomorrow's European Championship qualifier. The pitch is mainly sand with sparse patches of grass and some reporters find broken glass and stones on the playing surface, which has drainage problems. Manager Eoin Hand insists that the surface is simply not suitable and asks the Maltese to transfer the match to the much smaller Marsa Stadium. His plea is ignored.

WEDNESDAY 29TH MARCH 1995

Ireland drop a point at home to their counterparts from the north in a European Championship qualifier at Landsdowne Road, where Iain Dowie's goal on 72 minutes cancels out Niall Quinn's opener for the hosts.

SATURDAY 30TH MARCH 1946

Eoin Hand, Irish international footballer and the predecessor to Jack Charlton as the country's national manager, is born. His playing career starts at Dundalk and Shelbourne before Hand signs for Drumcondra, where he proves a great success and is signed in October 1986 by Portsmouth for £8,000. He spends most of the next decade at Pompey, earning 19 caps for Ireland, before becoming player-manager at Limerick, where his success prompts the FAI to give him the national job in 1979. Ireland narrowly miss out on qualification to the 1982 World Cup but results peter out. He resigns after failure to qualify for the 1984 European Championships and later manages Huddersfield Town and Shelbourne.

WEDNESDAY 30TH MARCH 1960

A first-half strike from captain Noel Cantwell, and another from Dermot Curtis, give Ireland a 2-0 win over Chile in a friendly at Dalymount Park watched by a 17,000 crowd.

WEDNESDAY 30TH MARCH 1977

A record crowd for an Irish football game of 48,000 floods into Lansdowne Road with Michel Platini's France the visitors for a vital World Cup qualifier. The size of the crowd is a surprise as the game is live on television. When French sweeper Christian Lopez heads out a free kick from Irish player-manager Johnny Giles, the French defence run out but the ball drops to Liam Brady who waltzes past Lopez and Bathenay for a famous goal. The result is Ireland's first World Cup win at Lansdowne Road. Platini played against Ireland in four World Cup matches; today's 1-0 defeat was the only time that he did not score.

WEDNESDAY 30TH MARCH 1983

Ireland's 200th match is played today in Malta, where a bumpy pitch at the stadium in Ta'Qali is a source of contention for Ireland. Frank Stapleton overcomes an ankle injury to start but a high wind makes life difficult for the visitors. Liam Brady, now at Sampdoria, is behind most of Ireland's best moves but Malta's goalkeeper John Bonello looks unbeatable. The 6,500 crowd are expecting Malta to earn a rare point until Stapleton scores in the last minute. "We came for two points and the Maltese were a bit unlucky to concede a goal in the last minute," Eoin Hand tells *The Times*. "[But] no-one can play on such a surface.

WEDNESDAY 31ST MARCH 1993

Ireland take on their counterparts from the North in a World Cup qualifier. Billy Bingham's side must get a result but no tickets have been sold to Northern Irish fans – an arrangement that will also see fans from the Republic unable to travel to Belfast for the final qualifier. Jack Charlton did not even see Ireland's last game – a 2-1 friendly win at home to Wales – preferring instead to watch Northern Ireland play Albania in a World Cup qualifier. Charlton has the match of Bingham today as his team cruise home as goals from Andy Townsend, Niall Quinn and Steve Staunton put Ireland 3-0 up inside half an hour and the score stays the same.

REPUBLIC OF IRELAND
On This Day

APRIL

WEDNESDAY 1st APRIL 2009

Giovanni Trapattoni returns to Italy with Ireland looking for points in today's World Cup qualifier in Bari. In a pulsating game, he gets a fine Irish performance and a result through Robbie Keane's 89th-minute equaliser. Ireland could have won but have to settle for a 1-1 draw. World Cup holders Italy leave the field to jeers. "I didn't want to say anything in the build-up because I didn't want to jinx it but we are among a select band of teams who have not been beaten in qualification," said Trapattoni to *The Guardian*. "I told the players, though, because I thought it would give them motivation. I cannot reproach them. They gave everything."

WEDNESDAY 2nd APRIL 1997

Ireland sport a garish orange away strip for the first time today that is rated the biggest Irish sporting dress disaster of all time by *The Times* – but that is not the reason that this date goes down in Irish history. Mick McCarthy had despatched the Macedonians easily enough the previous October, winning 3-0 at Lansdowne Road, but Skopje is another story. Alan McLoughlin gives Ireland the lead after eight minutes but in one of the worst performances of the Mick McCarthy era, the Macedonians win 3-2. To compound a dreadful performance and the loss of three World Cup qualifying points, Jason McAteer is sent off in the 90th minute. To commemorate the game, the worst player at Irish training sessions is forced to wear a jersey with 'I had a Macedonia' emblazoned on the front to mark this woeful nadir.

THURSDAY 3rd APRIL 1930

The birthday of Jack Fitzgerald, who would go on to win two caps for Ireland in 1955/56 and score on his debut against the Netherlands. He played for his local side Waterford originally as a half-back but switched to centre forward in the 1951/52 season and went on to score more than 100 goals in his career. Fitzgerald also represented Ireland at amateur level and played for the LOI representative XI. He left Waterford in 1964 and featured briefly for Cork Hibs but never went full-time, preferring to combine football with his job as a milkman. He died on November 23rd 2003, aged 73.

TUESDAY 4th APRIL 1978

Gerry Peyton faces a last-minute dash to Ireland today after Walsall refuse to release Irish number one Mick Kearns.

WEDNESDAY 4th APRIL 1984

Eoin Hand fields one of his strongest Irish teams in some time in Tel Aviv only to suffer a major setback. Eli Ohanna puts Israel ahead after just three minutes. Ireland dominate for long periods, prompted by Liam Brady in midfield, but are unable to find a way round Arie Haviv in the Israel goal and finish up crushed 3-0.

SUNDAY 5th APRIL 1953

Ireland lose 3-0 to England in an international youth tournament and finish the competition in sixth place.

SUNDAY 5th APRIL 1959

A crowd of 42,000 have flooded into Dalymount Park to see Ireland's first game in the new Nations Cup competition. Only 17 countries entered, with the British Home Nations not among them. To reduce the knockout competition to an even number, Ireland face Czechoslovakia in a two-legged preliminary round. Liam Tuohy puts Ireland ahead after 22 minutes and when Belgian referee Lucien Van Nuffel points to the spot 20 minutes later, Noel Cantwell does not miss. The visitors do not respond, giving Ireland a vital 2-0 victory to take to Bratislava for next month's second leg.

WEDNESDAY 5th APRIL 1978

Player-manager Johnny Giles opens the scoring for Ireland just three minutes into today's friendly with Turkey at Lansdowne Road. More goals from Paul McGee and a brace from Ray Treacy leave Ireland four goals clear at the break. Turkey rally and score twice in the second half, but lose 4-2.

MONDAY 6th APRIL 2009

Former Ireland manager Brian Kerr is confirmed as the new manager of the Faroe Islands. "It will be a very interesting and difficult challenge, but one I look forward to getting my teeth into," Kerr tells RTÉ. He was most recently working for St Patrick's Athletic and signs a contract to the end of 2011.

TUESDAY 7TH APRIL 1936

The birthday of Mick McGrath, who started out with Home Farm but moved to England in the summer of 1954 and signed for Blackburn Rovers. He made more than 260 appearances for the Ewood Park side, helping Blackburn win promotion to the First Division and into the final of the 1960 FA Cup, where McGrath scored an own goal in a 3-0 defeat to Wolves. His first Irish cap came against Austria in May 1958 and he went on to win 21 more caps. In 1966, McGrath joined Bradford Park Avenue, then worked for a brewery after hanging up his boots.

SUNDAY 8TH APRIL 1934

Victory over the Netherlands today will take Ireland to the World Cup finals in only their tenth international. There were five changes from the Irish XI that drew 4-4 at home to Belgium in their first World Cup qualifier two months earlier. Billy Kennedy of St. James's Gate, and Aberdeen's Paddy Moore, are the only forwards to retain their places. A 38,000 crowd at Amsterdam's Olympic Stadium is the biggest that Ireland have played in front of but no-one is overawed. The game is goalless until the 40th minute, when Kick Smit opens the scoring. Shelbourne's Johnny Squires quickly equalises but Billy Jordan then takes a knock and cannot continue. Substitutions are not part of the Irish game but are permitted outside the British Isles and Irish trainer Bill Lacey takes advantage of the 'Continental rule' to replace the injured Bohemians player with his club colleague Fred Horlacher. Ireland start the second half the stronger team and Paddy Moore scores his seventh goal in four internationals to give Ireland the lead. The Dutch, who are coached by former Bolton half-back Bob Glendenning, gain parity. The Irish are very much in the game until the 78th minute when, in a devastating seven-minute spell, the Dutch seal a 5-2 win and a place in the World Cup finals.

SUNDAY 8TH APRIL 1962

Goalkeeper Alan Kelly is injured just 34 minutes into Ireland's friendly with Austria at Dalymount Park. Dinny Lowry of St Patrick's comes off the bench for his debut but lets in three goals as Ireland go down 3-2. Noel Cantwell and Bill Tuohy get the home goals.

WEDNESDAY 8TH APRIL 1964

Before the first leg of their European Nations Cup quarter-final, Spain cancelled the entire La Liga programme to allow proper time for preparation and crush the Irish 5-1. In the return leg at Dalymount Park today, 38,100 fans see if Ireland can at least regain some pride but two goals from Pedro Marin complete a 7-1 aggregate win for the visitors. "Let it be understood that these forbearing footballers drawn from all four divisions in England have justified the 'misfits' tag," writes Tom Muldowney in *World Soccer*. "[They] do not represent soccer in the republic. [There are] exceptions, of course: Hurley, Cantwell, Kelly and McEvoy, [who are] worthy standard bearers."

TUESDAY 9TH APRIL 1961

Michael Kennedy, who was born today, played for ten different clubs in the Football League, staying longest at Portsmouth, where he makes more than 120 appearances in a three-year spell starting in 1984. During this period, he broke into the Irish set-up and gained two caps towards the end of Jack Charlton's reign in 1986 but was never called up by his successor, Mick McCarthy.

SUNDAY 10TH APRIL 1983

Paul Green is born in Pontefract. He spends the first nine years of his career at Doncaster Rovers but only breaks into the Ireland team after moving to Derby County in 2008. His grandmother is Irish and he is called into Giovanni Trapattoni's training camp in May 2010 and makes his debut later that month against Paraguay as a second-half substitute.

THURSDAY 11TH APRIL 1974

Matt Holland is born today. An industrious midfielder, in three years at West Ham United, he never made a first-team appearance and at the start of the 1995/96 season signed for an AFC Bournemouth side seemingly doomed to relegation from the third tier of English football. The move made Holland's career. He is made captain under Mel Machin and the Cherries forge a miraculous escape. In 1997, Holland is signed by Ipswich Town for £800,000 and breaks into the Irish team two years later, going on to win 49 caps and playing in the 2002 World Cup finals.

FRIDAY 11TH APRIL 2008

Ireland's futsal team make history by winning only their second competitive match in the short-sided version of the game. In qualifiers for the 2008 Uefa championship finals, Ireland lost 6-2 to the Netherlands on their debut a few days earlier but beat Azerbaijan 4-3 today.

WEDNESDAY 12TH APRIL 1978

Poland, always Poland. Some Irish internationals felt half their caps were won against the Poles, who play Ireland for the third time in a year in Lodz. All three games are friendlies and Ireland have yet to lose until today, when Gerry Peyton ruins his outstanding display by gifting Zbigniew Boniek an opener on 52 minutes. Poland win 3-0.

SUNDAY 12TH APRIL 1981

Liam Brady scores his eighth goal of the season for Juventus in a 3-1 win over strugglers AC Pistoiese.

TUESDAY 13TH APRIL 1954

The Irish lose 3-1 to Spain in an international youth tournament in West Germany. Ireland do not progress from a group also including Portugal and Yugoslavia, and lose to France 2-0 in the consolation tournament.

THURSDAY 14TH APRIL 1960

Liam Buckley broke into Shelbourne's first XI at 18 and then the Irish under-21 team, winning his first cap against England. After joining Shamrock Rovers, he won his first Irish cap against Poland in 1984. Before his next Irish cap, he spent a spell with Belgian side Waregem, then returned to Shamrock Rovers and appeared for Ireland again in 1985 under Eoin Hand.

TUESDAY 15TH APRIL 2008

Wayne Rooney's younger brother could make his international debut... for Ireland. A 17-year-old midfielder with Macclesfield Town, John Rooney is reportedly considering taking advantage of his Irish heritage to join the Republic. "I've never heard of two brothers playing for different countries before, so this would be a footballing boundary crossed," former Irish favourite Tony Cascarino tells Sky News Online: "If John is anything like Wayne, we'll be delighted to have him play for us."

MONDAY 16TH APRIL 1979

Johnny Giles resigns as Ireland manager.

SATURDAY 17TH APRIL 1948

The Republic of Ireland's youth team take on their counterparts from the North at Europe's first international youth tournament. The competition staged in England also included the hosts, Austria, Belgium, Italy, the Netherlands and Wales. After losing to eventual finalists the Netherlands 2-0 in their opener, the Irish saw off Austria 1-0 the previous day to set up today's game with Northern Ireland, which the Republic win 2-0 to clinch fifth place.

WEDNESDAY 17TH APRIL 2002

Mick McCarthy substitutes eight players in today's friendly with the US at Lansdowne Road, where goals from Mark Kinsella and Gary Doherty give Ireland a 2-1 win in a friendly.

SUNDAY 18TH APRIL 2010

Glasgow Celtic's Aiden McGeady could become the first Irish international to play professionally in Russia after giants Spartak Moscow express interest in signing the midfielder.

FRIDAY 19TH APRIL 1957

Liam Whelan has not scored for a dozen matches but the Manchester United and Ireland forward rediscovers his scoring touch today by notching up a hat-trick for his club side in a First Division game with Burnley.

SATURDAY 20TH APRIL 1929

Ireland have only played four internationals but win for the second time in a row today as Belgium, victims in their last game a year ago in Liege, are thrashed at Dalymount Park in the first game at the home of Bohemians. On his debut, John Burke is made captain. Belgium had scored 16 goals in eight games since last meeting Ireland but dashing centre forward Raymond Braine could find no way through the Irish defence today. John Joe Flood opens the scoring two minutes before half-time and the game remains close until Shelbourne's David Byrne latches onto a long punt up-field to add a second. Last-minute goals from Flood give the Shamrock Rovers' player his hat-trick and Ireland a 4-0 win.

PLAYERS FROM EUROPE'S FIRST INTERNATIONAL YOUTH TOURNAMENT STAGED IN ENGLAND IN 1948 AND FEATURING THE REPUBLIC OF IRELAND. COURTESY OF THE FOOTBALL ASSOCIATION

THURSDAY 20TH APRIL 1967

Alan McLoughlin is born on this day. He joins Manchester United as a youngster but cannot make the first XI and plays in the lower leagues for Swindon Town, where he first makes the Irish team. He also plays for Torquay United, Southampton and Aston Villa before joining Portsmouth in 1992, where he makes more than 300 appearances. He is first called up for Ireland by Jack Charlton, making his debut in 1990 in a 3-0 win in Malta, and goes on to win 42 caps.

TUESDAY 20TH APRIL 1976

Ireland's most-capped player is Shay Given, who was born today in Lifford, County Donegal. Given, who shares a birthday with another of Ireland's most-capped players, Steve Finnan, signed for Glasgow Celtic, then managed by Irish legend Liam Brady, as a youth but leaves without making the first team for Blackburn Rovers in 1994. He has loans at Swindon Town and Sunderland, where he is playing on his Ireland debut against Russia in March 1996. The following year, he signs permanently for Newcastle United and makes more than 350 appearances for the club. In February 2009, Manchester City pay £5.9 million for Given, who was only 30-odd games short of beating Newcastle's appearance record. He played in the 2002 World Cup finals and has made more than 100 appearances for Ireland – joining Kevin Kilbane and Steve Staunton in passing the 100-cap mark.

WEDNESDAY 21ST APRIL 1971

Johnny Giles quits his post as manager of West Bromwich Albion.

SATURDAY 21ST APRIL 2001

Nursing a grudge from a game four years previously, Roy Keane hacks down Alf-Inge Haaland of Leeds United, while playing for Manchester United at Old Trafford. In his own autobiography in 2002, Keane recalls: "I'd waited long enough. I f****** hit him hard. The ball was there (I think). 'Take that, you c***. And don't ever stand over me again sneering about fake injuries. And tell your pal [David] Wetherall there's some for him as well.' I didn't wait for Mr Elleray to show the red card. I turned and walked to the dressing room." Haaland's career never recovered.

WEDNESDAY 22ND APRIL 1998

Two times World Cup winners Argentina visit Lansdowne Road, where a crowd of 38,500 see Mick McCarthy's team undone by two first-half goals from Gabriel Batistuta and Ariel Ortega, respectively. Mick McCarthy's team try to take the game to Argentina in the second half but go down 2-0.

SATURDAY 23RD APRIL 1927

At 37 years and 211 days old, Wexford's Bill Lacy becomes the oldest man to play for Ireland. After providing the Irish with their international debut the previous year, Italy had promised to come to Dublin for a rematch. The only problem was that someone in Italy forgot that the Italians had committed to play France in Paris the next day – so a B team is sent to Lansdowne Road. Ireland took the lead after just six minutes through Bob Fullam of Shamrock Rovers but the Italian second string includes a forward line that scored 60 goals that season. Italy revive and two second-half goals seal a 2-1 win for the visitors in front of a 20,000 crowd.

WEDNESDAY 23RD APRIL 1986

Two goals inside a minute settle today's game between Ireland and Uruguay. Gerry Daly opens the scoring on 22 minutes but moments later Mick McCarthy puts the ball past Packie Bonner for a 1-1 draw at Lansdowne Road.

SUNDAY 24TH APRIL 1949

Ireland slump to a 2-0 defeat at home to Belgium in a friendly at Dalymount Park watched by 40,000 spectators.

SUNDAY 24TH APRIL 1977

Johnny Giles is left frustrated after Poland hold off Ireland for a 0-0 draw in a friendly international at Dalymount Park

TUESDAY 24TH APRIL 2001

FAI chief executive Bernard O'Byrne resigns after opposition to the Eircom Park stadium project. "From my point of view he was professional and likeable and was good to me, both professionally and personally," wrote Irish manager Mick McCarthy.

WEDNESDAY 25TH APRIL 1990

Steve Staunton gives Ireland a 1-0 win over the Soviet Union at a packed Lansdowne Road with a goal on 59 minutes.

WEDNESDAY 25TH APRIL 2001

Ildefons Lima, one of Andorra's few professionals, stuns a 35,000 Lansdowne Road crowd by opening the scoring as he nods home a Justo Ruiz free kick. Andorra are uncontrollable and for the next three minutes Mick McCarthy's team are losing to a Pyrenean mountain-top at home until Kevin Kilbane edges a Matt Holland free kick home. Two minutes later and Ireland are in front as Mark Kinsella crashes home a Gary Doherty shot that rebounds off the crossbar. Gary Breen adds another on 76 minutes.

SUNDAY 26TH APRIL 1931

Ireland will play many famous games against Spain and that rivalry starts today, when Irish captain John Joe Flood leads his team out at the Montjuich Stadium in Barcelona. Spain are widely viewed as the top side in international football and became the first team outside the British Isles to beat England two years earlier. With the exceptions of Tom Farquharson of Cardiff City and Glasgow Celtic's Peter Kavanagh, the Irish team was drawn mostly from the LOI and is expected to lose. A performance by Ireland that was described by one Spanish newspaper as "cold and calculating" saw the visitors take the lead on 34 minutes through Paddy Moore of Shamrock Rovers. Angel Arocha of Athletic Madrid equalised three minutes later but Ireland held on for a 1-1 draw.

WEDNESDAY 26TH APRIL 1989

There is a rebellion among the Irish players, who before today's World Cup qualifier with Spain refuse to attend a post-game function for sponsors Opel. A win today over group favourites Spain will take the Irish closer than ever to qualification. Stunned by the recent Hillsborough disaster, John Aldridge is given compassionate leave by Jack Charlton and Frank Stapleton takes his place. In front of 49,600 fans at Lansdowne Road, Stapleton pressures Michel to put the ball past Andoni Zubizarreta in the Spanish goal after only 15 minutes. Spain up the tempo but Ireland's 4-5-1 formation holds firm to prevail 1-0.

WEDNESDAY 26TH APRIL 1995

An own goal on the stroke of half-time by Vitor Baia gives Ireland a vital 1-0 win over Portugal in a European Championship qualifier at Lansdowne Road. The game is perhaps the last great performance of Jack Charlton's era as the next fixture is in Liechtenstein…

WEDNESDAY 26TH APRIL 2000

Ravaged by injuries, Mick McCarthy hands debuts to Steve Finnan, Richard Dunne, Barry Quinn, Alan Mahon and Gary Doherty but Vassilios Lakis's goal wins the game for Greece.

THURSDAY 26TH APRIL 2007

Former Irish international Steve Heighway ends a relationship with Liverpool that started 37 years ago when he resigns from his post as the club's youth-team manager after his charges won the FA Youth Cup.

THURSDAY 27TH APRIL 1933

Liam Tuohy, who was born today in Dublin, was an outside-left for Shamrock Rovers and Newcastle United and won eight caps for Ireland before moving into club management in the LOI. Tuohy takes the part-time manager's job of Ireland, which pays £500 a year, in 1971. In his first game in charge in October that year, Ireland are trounced 6-0 by Austria in a European Championship qualifier. He resigned after just 11 games but in the 1980s proved far more successful with the Irish under-19 team, who qualified for three European Championships and one World Cup finals.

THURSDAY 27TH APRIL 1972

Johnny Giles is named as captain of an Ireland squad that will travel to Brazil for a tournament this summer.

WEDNESDAY 28TH APRIL 1982

Eoin Hand's side visit Algiers for a friendly with an Algerian side that will prove one of the surprise packages at this summer's World Cup finals in Spain. The Algerians give notice of that promise with a fine 2-0 win over Ireland who are missing Tony Galvin and Chris Hughton, whose club side Spurs refuse to let the pair travel.

WEDNESDAY 28TH APRIL 1993

Ireland's World Cup qualifying campaign is building momentum with three wins and two draws from five games as European champions Denmark visit Dublin and put a dampener on Jack Charlton's enthusiasm. Ireland draw saves from Peter Schmeichel but after 28 minutes Lars Olsen sends a long ball downfield that Paul McGrath opts to head instead of leaving to Packie Bonner. The ball drops to Kim Vilfort who volleys past Bonner. Denmark dig in until Niall Quinn rescues a point 15 minutes from time by heading home Steve Staunton's cross. "All in all then, the pressure is beginning on every side as we head towards the halfway stage of our programme," reflected Charlton. "It doesn't get any easier."

SUNDAY 29TH APRIL 1956

Kevin Bernard Moran is born today and grew up in the Rialto district of Dublin. An accomplished Gaelic footballer, he won two All-Ireland Senior Championships with Dublin and was playing the association game with Dublin Pegasus when Manchester United manager Dave Sexton signed Moran in 1978. He stays with the Old Trafford club for a decade, making more than 230 appearances and winning 71 caps for Ireland after making his debut in a 2-0 defeat against Switzerland in 1980. His best form comes under Jack Charlton. Moran plays in Euro 88 and the 1990 World Cup finals and travelled to the 1994 World Cup finals at 38 only for injury to rule him out. He also played for Sporting Gijon and Blackburn Rovers and retired in 1994.

WEDNESDAY 29TH APRIL 1981

Ronnie Whelan makes his debut by replacing Gerry Daly 63 minutes into a 3-1 friendly win over Czechoslovakia, thus emulating his father Ronnie Whelan senior, who won two caps for Ireland in the early 1960s. Six other sets of fathers and sons have played for Ireland over the years: Jack and Fionan Fagan; Jimmy and Tommy Dunne; Con and Mick Martin; John and Mick Lawlor; Don and Terry Donovan; and Alan Kelly senior and his son of the same name.

WEDNESDAY 29TH APRIL 1987

Belgium hold Ireland to a 0-0 draw at Lansdowne Road in a European Championship qualifier.

FRIDAY 30TH APRIL 1954

Gerry Daly, who is born today in Cabra, Dublin, signed for Manchester United from Bohemians for a fee believed to be around £20,000 before he was even 19. But, in his first season at Old Trafford, the club were relegated. After four years at Old Trafford, he leaves in 1977 for Derby County. Daly's first taste of the international game was a B international with England in 1976, when he was Ireland's star in a 1-1 draw, scoring the only goal from the penalty spot. He makes his full debut the same year and goes on to win 48 caps for Ireland, scoring 18 goals. A dashing midfielder, his best form comes under Eoin Hand and he was part of the team that narrowly missed out on the 1982 World Cup finals.

WEDNESDAY 30TH APRIL 1980

Alan Kelly senior's sole match as Ireland manager comes today. Johnny Giles has just quit and Kelly, his number two, steps up for today's 2-0 friendly win over Switzerland, Don Givens and Gerry Daly scoring. Eoin Hand has been appointed as Kelly's assistant but after one game the former international keeper accepts that his full-time job at Preston North End comes first and stands down.

THURSDAY 30TH APRIL 1981

The birthday of John Francis O'Shea, a stylish defender and sometimes midfielder with Manchester United, who started out in the LOI with Waterford. In 2000 he spent a brief spell on loan at AFC Bournemouth, then was loaned again the next year to Belgian side Royal Antwerp, but O'Shea has gone on to make more than 200 appearances for Manchester United, winning numerous medals. His Ireland debut came in a friendly with Croatia in 2001 only for O'Shea to give away a penalty in injury time that saw the Irish pegged back to 2-2. He remains an international regular with more than half a century of caps.

WEDNESDAY 30TH APRIL 1997

Ireland's last match – the pitiful 3-2 defeat in Macedonia – is followed by another loss today. Three more World Cup qualifying points are gone but the performance in a 1-0 defeat to Romania in Bucharest is at least better.

REPUBLIC OF IRELAND
On This Day

MAY

WEDNESDAY 1st MAY 1985

Ireland have scored four goals in their last ten games as Norway arrive at Lansdowne Road for a World Cup qualifier. With just two points out of a possible six, Ireland are not much of a draw and only 15,000 spectators turn up to see a feeble showing with Norway holding out for a 0-0 draw. Seven minutes from the end, Paul McGrath comes on for his debut. Downcast at Ireland's poor showing, manager Eoin Hand tells his players in the privacy of the dressing room that he intends to quit but they change his mind – for now...

FRIDAY 2nd MAY 1958

David Anthony O'Leary is born in north London and grows up in Dublin, where he plays for Shelbourne as a youth before being snapped up by Arsenal, joining as an apprentice in 1973. After making his first XI debut two years later, O'Leary goes on to make more than 550 appearances for the Gunners before leaving in 1993. After 68 run-outs for Ireland, he retires from international football and makes a handful of appearances for Leeds United before moving into club management with the Yorkshire outfit, then Aston Villa.

WEDNESDAY 2nd MAY 1979

The qualifiers for the 1980 European Championship finals start with three draws in a row for Ireland but that ends today when a goal a minute from half-time by Gerry Daly, and another from Don Givens on 66 minutes at Lansdowne Road, give the Irish a win over Austria.

SUNDAY 3rd MAY 1936

Ireland begin their second European tour against Hungary, who have lost just 14 out of 92 matches at home. On a sunny day in Budapest, Ireland utilise the long-ball to combat Hungary's short-passing game. The tactic works to good effect. Arsenal's Jimmy Dunne blasts past Antal Szabo to wipe out an earlier Hungarian strike and Joe O'Reilly gives Ireland a shock half-time lead that disappears minutes into the second half when Con Moulson gives away a penalty but Dunne restores Ireland's advantage. A downpour then changes the conditions and Sas saves face for Hungary with an equaliser 15 minutes from time for a 3-3 draw.

WEDNESDAY 3RD MAY 1961

Scotland have qualified for the last two World Cup finals but Ireland are unlikely to emulate that achievement after their first qualifier for the 1962 competition in Chile. Scotland crush the Irish at Hampden Park today. Two goals down at the break, Joe Haverty reduces the deficit but Scotland run out comfortable 4-1 winners but a young Johnny Giles shows great promise.

SUNDAY 4TH MAY 1969

Paddy Mulligan and Mick Leech are handed debuts as Ireland take on Czechoslovakia in a World Cup qualifier at Dalymount Park. The Shamrock Rovers duo are joined by teammate Frank O'Neill in the starting line-up and a fourth LOI player, Limerick's Al Finucane. Ireland had beaten their visitors in their last game, a Nations Cup match that had eliminated the Czechs, who get vengeance today. Eamon Rogers scores first on 15 minutes but in a cynically brutal performance, Czechoslovakia literally hammer Ireland. Leech is stretchered off after a dreadful over-the-ball challenge. Substitutes are now allowed in World Cup qualifiers and Eoin Hand comes on but the visitors have the momentum. Second-half goals from Kabat and Adamec win the game 2-1.

SUNDAY 5TH MAY 1935

Ireland take on Switzerland for the first time looking for their first victory in three years but Paddy Gaskins' side go down 1-0 in Basel to a 62nd-minute penalty by Walter Weiler of Grasshoppers.

WEDNESDAY 5TH MAY 1965

Four Manchester United players help drive Ireland to one of their best results in years. Spain are the visitors at Dalymount Park, where a 40,000-plus crowd come to see if Ireland can improve on their last dismal attempt to qualify for the World Cup finals. Shay Brennan, Pat and Tony Dunne and captain Noel Cantwell journey over from Old Trafford. When Cantwell jumps for a ball with Jose Iribar, the Spanish keeper – under pressure also from his own defender, Ignacio Zoco – spills the ball into his own net on 63 minutes. Spain flood forward and Jesus Glaria misses a sitter but Ireland hold on for a magnificent 1-0 win over the 1964 European champions.

SUNDAY 5TH MAY 1974

Ireland are downed 2-1 by Brazil in Rio de Janeiro at the Maracana in a game that Steve Heighway will not forget. The Liverpool star was not even in Brazil – Terry Mancini gets Ireland's consolation at the Maracana – but Heighway is vilified in the media after turning down a chance to go on the end of season trip. "I don't need to be told I came in for some criticism over that – people told me to my face that they thought I should have gone," he admits in his autobiography, *Liverpool: My Team*. "But it simply wasn't a case of my not being bothered about going on the trip. I had a really gruelling season with Liverpool, and I felt physically and mentally shattered. In fact, I'd been waiting since Christmas for that season to end, and I knew that if I agreed to go to Brazil I could easily have let people down, because I wouldn't have been able to do myself justice."

SATURDAY 6TH MAY 1972

Johnny Giles plays in the Leeds United team that beat Arsenal 1-0 today in the 100th FA Cup Final, at Wembley Stadium.

WEDNESDAY 7TH MAY 1952

Ireland suffer an almighty caning at the hands of Austria in a friendly in Vienna, as the hosts – four goals up at the interval – record a resounding 6-0 win.

SUNDAY 7TH MAY 1961

A chance that Ireland could go to next year's World Cup finals virtually ends today as Scotland stroll to a 3-0 win in front of a 36,000 crowd at Dalymount Park. Having been crushed 4-1 in Scotland only four days earlier, the Irish XI leave the field to jeers.

TUESDAY 7TH MAY 2002

A fortnight before Fifa's deadline, Mick McCarthy shows his hand early and announces his squad for next month's World Cup finals in Japan and South Korea. "I have dreamed of this day ever since I was appointed Irish manager back in 1996," says McCarthy in his World Cup diary.

SUNDAY 8th MAY 1932

Ireland played the Netherlands in the quarter-finals of the Olympic Games eight years ago but that game does not count as a full international. Today is the first of many clashes between the sides. The trip to the Amsterdam Olympic Stadium via Holyhead, Dover and the Hook of Holland is torturous. Captain Mick O'Brien, playing in England with Watford, leads his side out against a team that had only won four of the last 25 games. On his international debut, Joe O'Reilly of Brideville gives Ireland the lead and Paddy Moore wraps up a comfortable 2-0 win.

WEDNESDAY 8th MAY 1935

Jack Charlton, the most successful manager in the history of the Irish national team, is born today in Ashington, northern England. He joins Leeds United in 1950 as a youth-team player and spends the next 22 years with the club, amassing more than 600 first XI appearances – and winning the World Cup with England in 1966 – before retiring in 1973. He moves into club management with Middlesbrough the same year, later managing Sheffield Wednesday and Newcastle United, before taking over Ireland in 1986 and staying for nine years. Under Charlton, Ireland qualify for the 1988 European Championships and two World Cup finals. He resigns after Ireland lose a play-off with Holland and fail to qualify for Euro 96 in England.

WEDNESDAY 8th MAY 1957

Ireland had only played England twice before and never at Wembley. The Irish surprisingly won their only fixture in England at Goodison Park in 1949. A repeat in today's World Cup qualifier at Wembley is never likely. Tommy Taylor of Manchester United scores past Drumcondra keeper Alan Kelly twice in the first 18 minutes. Twenty minutes later, Kelly defies Tom Finney but John Atyeo heads in the rebound and two minutes later Taylor has his hat-trick, heading home a Finney corner. The Irish start the second half in brighter fashion, pulling a goal back as Atyeo's Bristol City teammate Dermot Curtis nods home a centre from Arsenal's Joe Haverty. In the dying moments, Atyeo adds another for a 5-1 win in a game that is the last played by 42-year-old Stanley Matthews at Wembley. Ireland will not return to the stadium for 19 years.

SUNDAY 8TH MAY 1988

Brian Kerr's Ireland win the Uefa under-16 championships in Scotland. Ireland strolled out of their group in top spot after drawing with the hosts and beating Finland and Spain. Ireland out do Denmark 2-0 in the quarter-finals then see off Portugal in the semi-finals thanks to two second-half goals from Shaun Byrne of Motherwell. In the final at McDiarmid Park in Perth, Ireland strike through Keith Foy. Italy equalise but David McMahan's goal on 57 minutes takes the title.

SATURDAY 9TH MAY 1936

Ireland's European tour ends today with a first game against Luxembourg. The Grand Duchy had lost 43 of their 67 internationals but were far more experienced with a total of 105 caps against 41 for Ireland. Arsenal's Jimmy Dunne opens the scoring on nine minutes but Luxembourg dig in and equalise in the second half through Leon Mart. Joey Donnelly regains the lead for the Irish before a Jimmy Kelly brace and another from Dunne, his seventh in just four internationals, see Ireland home 5-1. When Jimmy Dunne gets back to London, he finds that he has been put on the transfer list by Arsenal.

SATURDAY 10TH MAY 1947

Johnny Carey leads a Rest of the World side that take on Great Britain and Northern Ireland in a match at Wembley Stadium aimed at raising funds for Fifa, whose coffers are bare after World War II. Before the game, the Rest of the World's keeper, French international Julien Darui, is advised by a 'health expert' to drink three glasses of wine plus added sugar to improve his performance. His teammates object, but Darui does as he is told. Sweden's Gunnar Nordhal nets for Carey's team but the hosts run riot, winning 6-1.

SUNDAY 10TH MAY 1959

Ireland's first dalliance with the new Nations Cup ends in the preliminary round as Czechoslovakia – who will go on to reach the semi-finals of this competition and the final of the 1962 World Cup – trounce their visitors. A 60,000 crowd in Bratislava roars as French referee Joseph Barberan awards a penalty after just three minutes and Imrich Stacho scores. Ireland won the first leg 2-0 and stay ahead on aggregate in a two-legged tie until the second half, when the Czechs romp home 4-0.

SUNDAY 11TH MAY 1930

Internationals will soon take up a larger space in the football calendar but today Ireland play only their fifth international in five years with a third game in a row against Belgium. The Belgians have yet to beat Ireland and succumb to a 3-1 defeat in Brussels, Jimmy Dunne of Sheffield United netting a brace and John Joe Flood scoring his fourth goal in three internationals. Dunne will not play for Ireland again for another six years.

SATURDAY 12TH MAY 1973

Chelsea manager Dave Sexton tells John Dempsey that he can leave the west London club after the Irish international missed most of the last season through injury.

WEDNESDAY 13TH MAY 1954

Scotland beat Ireland 2-0 in a youth international.

SUNDAY 13TH MAY 1973

Liam Tuohy has announced he will quit his job as Ireland manager at the end of the current World Cup qualifying series due to 'business pressures'. Only two fixtures remain. Ireland lost to the Soviet Union at home earlier in the qualifiers but come close to revenge today against a side including the debutant Oleg Blokhin. Ireland are on the back foot but the hosts only have Onischenko's goal on 58 minutes to show for all that pressure.

SATURDAY 13TH MAY 1978

Ireland play in the semi-finals of an international competition for the first time. The Uefa Amateur Cup was a short-lived attempt to revive the amateur ethos. The Republic lost three out of four qualifiers on entering the first tournament in 1967 and sat out the next two championships in 1970 and 1974 before re-entering for the final competition in 1978. Withdrawals meant that only the Netherlands stood between the Irish and a semi-final place. After following up a 2-1 win in Dublin in March 1977 with a 2-2 draw in Waalwijk two months later, the Irish booked their place in the four-team finals in Athens. In their semi-final today, Ireland are undone 2-0 by hosts Greece and then thrashed 3-0 in the third-place play-off by West Germany.

TUESDAY 14TH MAY 1957

Alan Kelly is one of four players from the Irish XI trounced 5-1 by England that are dropped in the team named today for the return at Dalymount Park. Tommy Godwin replaces Kelly, Seamus Dunne comes in at right-back for Don Donovan, Ron Nolan replaces ousted captain Peter Farrell, and Charlie Hurley is handed his debut in place of Gerry Mackey.

SATURDAY 14TH MAY 1988

Ireland's John Aldridge becomes the first player to miss a penalty in an FA Cup Final, when Wimbledon's Dave Beasant saves his spot kick. Liverpool lose 1-0.

TUESDAY 14TH MAY 2002

Niall Quinn's Sunderland take on Mick McCarthy's Republic of Ireland at the Stadium of Light in a testimonial for the Irish striker. Goals from Mark Kennedy, David Connolly and a Kevin Kilbane header produce a 3-0 win for Ireland. A 36,000 crowd raises £1 million, which Quinn donates to charity.

THURSDAY 15TH MAY 1980

Crystal Palace midfielder Jerry Murphy pulls out of Ireland's prestigious friendly with Argentina tomorrow due to a bout of tonsillitis. Murphy only has three caps for Ireland and never plays again.

FRIDAY 16TH MAY 1980

"There are only two certainties in life. People die and football managers get the sack," says Eoin Hand, who starts his career today with a match that pits his new charges against World Cup holders Argentina. Diego Maradona missed that triumph but is in the Argentine XI that lines up against the Irish at Lansdowne Road, where a 35,000 crowd see Jose Daniel Valencia's 28th-minute goal settle the match.

THURSDAY 16TH MAY 2002

Ireland play their final warm-up game before leaving for Japan and the World Cup. Fellow World Cup finalists Nigeria triumph 2-1 at Lansdowne Road but Ireland manager Mick McCarthy is not too bothered. "It is the Irish players' performance, individually and collectively, that is important to me," he writes in *Ireland's World Cup 2002*.

MONDAY 17TH MAY 1937

The only other visit by Ireland to Basel's Wankdorf Stadium produced a 1-0 defeat to Switzerland two years earlier but a first-half goal from Jimmy Dunne, now at Southampton, reverses that scoreline today in front of a 16,000 crowd.

TUESDAY 17TH MAY 1988

Paul McGrath's testimonial is played at Lansdowne Road and realises record gate receipts of £600,000 as 39,000 fans watch a Jack Charlton XI beat a Republic of Ireland XI 3-2.

FRIDAY 17TH MAY 2002

"This has been the light at the end of the tunnel from some very hectic weeks," says Mick McCarthy as the Ireland manager and his team board an Aer Lingus flight to Amsterdam, and then on to Narita Aiport to reach their base at Saipan, in Japan, for the World Cup finals.

THURSDAY 18TH MAY 1939

Ireland's 2-2 draw in Cork with Hungary in their last match was a surprise but Jimmy Dunne's team repeat the feat against the 1938 World Cup finalists as Kevin O'Flanagan of Bohemians twice pegs back the hosts. The game was watched by a crowd of 15,000 at the MTK Stadium in Budapest.

SATURDAY 18TH MAY 1985

Ireland international Kevin Moran becomes the first player to be sent off in an FA Cup Final at Wembley, when the Manchester United defender sees red for a professional foul on Everton's Peter Reid. Manchester United still win 1-0, courtesy of Norman Whiteside's goal.

WEDNESDAY 18TH MAY 1988

The Irish Olympic team play their last-ever competitive match, a respectable 2-2 draw with Spain in Albacete, with Dundalk's Barry Kehoe and Noel Larkin of Shamrock Rovers scoring the goals. After the 1988 Games in Seoul, qualification is decided through under-21 teams and Ireland do not need a separate Olympic XI again after today's match.

SATURDAY 18TH MAY 2002

Ireland's attempt to win the Four Nations tournament for non-professional players fails at the last. Ireland, England, Scotland and Wales have committed to playing annually and this first championship is held in Lincolnshire. Ireland beat Scotland 2-0 on May 14th through goals from Arkins and Molloy, then see off England 2-1 two days later with a Molloy brace. But in the title decider today, Wales romp home 5-2.

SUNDAY 19TH MAY 1957

A mere 11 days after suffering a 5-1 hammering at Wembley, Ireland face England in a rematch. England have six points from three World Cup qualifiers, Ireland two. But by winning their last two games, the Irish can force a play-off as goal difference does not count. Noel Cantwell and Billy Wright lead out the teams at Dalymount Park in front of a record 47,600 crowd. Fans are still struggling through the turnstiles as Ireland roar into action and many miss Alf Ringstead's third-minute opener for the hosts. Tommy Godwin later proves Ireland's hero with a series of brave saves but Peter Atyeo wrecks Ireland's World Cup dreams with a last-minute equaliser.

SATURDAY 19TH MAY 1973

A win in Paris today would just keep Irish World Cup hopes alive in Liam Tuohy's last game as manager. France would also then need to win their next match in Russia and Tuohy's team win their first away point in 16 years as Mick Martin's header on 84 minutes rescues a 1-1 draw but Ireland are out.

SATURDAY 19TH MAY 1979

Ireland go down 1-0 to Bulgaria in Sofia in a European Championship qualifier that leaves Jimmy Holmes with a horrific broken leg. The cast is put on too tight and Holmes starts losing consciousness, forcing Ireland's plane to stop off in Switzerland for medical help. He later plays for Vancouver Whitecaps, Leicester City, Brentford, Torquay United and Peterborough United but only won one more Irish cap after the injury sustained in this game. Holmes later joined the police in the Midlands and once put his boots back on after a player did not show up for a testimonial.

WEDNESDAY 20TH MAY 2009

Alan Kelly Sr., Irish goalkeeping legend, passes away in the United States, aged 72. A player for Bray, Drumcondra and Preston North End in England, he won 47 caps for Ireland and his sons Alan junior and Gary also became professional goalkeepers. FAI president David Blood said, "Alan Kelly senior was a former record caps holder and a great servant to Irish football. He started his playing career in the League of Ireland before moving to Preston North End where he made a club-record 514 appearances and became a legend at Deepdale where the Town End was named in his honour in 2001. With the passing of Alan Kelly Sr., we have lost one of Ireland's greatest-ever goalkeepers."

TUESDAY 21ST MAY 1923

Media reports claim that an application by the IFSFA – the forerunner of the FAI – to join Fifa that went before the world body's annual congress yesterday in Switzerland has been rejected after Home Nations' opposition. The reports prove unfounded. The Home Nations, though powerful, are no longer in Fifa and providing the British Foreign Office confirm the political status of the Free State by September 1st, the Irish will be admitted to Fifa.

SUNDAY 21ST MAY 1967

A torrential downpour sees just 6,257 fans turn up for Ireland's European Championship qualifier with Czechoslovakia at Dalymount Park, the smallest crowd for an international for years. Those few fans braving the weather see little to enthuse about as Ireland go down 2-0. "In addition to it being the worst attended international, it also ranks as the poorest played," wrote Tom Muldowney in *World Soccer*. "Few of the players reached club standard, the majority played as if they hated every game of football, serving up 90 minutes of miss and mess to the handful of drenched supporters who told them in harsh terms – and slow handclap – what they thought of their lack of effort."

TUESDAY 21ST MAY 2002

Roy Keane tells Mick McCarthy that he wants to leave Ireland's squad in Saipan for the 2002 World Cup before a game has even been played. McCarthy tells only a handful of people before going to bed…

FRIDAY 21st MAY 2010

Irish centre-half Shane Duffy nearly dies after a freak training-ground accident lacerates the Everton teenager's liver, causing severe internal bleeding. Duffy is treated on the pitch by Professor John Byrne then taken to Mater Hospital for an emergency operation. Byrne tells *The Observer*: "It was a freak injury that in another 100 years of medicine we may never see again. [The hospital's] expertise and fast response saved Shane's life."

SUNDAY 22nd MAY 1938

'The ball is too soft' is not a grievance heard too often during internationals but that is Ireland's complaint after going in 3-0 down to Poland in Warsaw. The Poles duly replace the ball and double the scoreline to 6-0 as Ireland suffer their biggest international defeat to date. The Poles had experienced more international defeats than victories but driven on by Gregor Wodarz, whose hat-trick two years earlier knocked Great Britain out of the Berlin Olympics, were too good for Ireland today – with either ball.

SUNDAY 22nd MAY 1966

Ireland play the first of two games on a brief European tour at a sun-soaked Prater Stadium in Vienna. Manager Johnny Carey is absent and Ireland are led jointly by Noel Cantwell of Manchester United and Sunderland's Charlie Hurley. Due to the heat, the game is played at a deathly slow pace and Ireland deserve a draw but Walter Seitl seizes on a short back pass from Mick McGrath and hammers the ball past Alan Kelly on 76 minutes for a 1-0 win.

SUNDAY 23rd MAY 1937

France were among the prime movers behind Fifa's formation in 1904 but do not take on Ireland until today. The two sides clash at the Colombes Stadium, scene of Ireland's heroics at the 1924 Olympic football tournament, and the Irish produce another memorable performance. France are to host next year's World Cup finals but have lost all four games this season and Ireland make that five. Jimmy Dunne scored eight goals in his previous five matches but strikes from Davy Jordan of Wolverhampton and Coventry City's Johnny Brown seal a 2-0 win.

TUESDAY 23RD MAY 1939

Ireland will not play an international for seven years after today's game with Germany. The Irish are on the second leg of a European tour that also took in Hungary, where a fine draw was secured. That result is repeated in Bremen. Germany had been eliminated in the first round of the previous year's World Cup by the Swiss and just lost to Luxembourg, so have something to prove to a 35,000 crowd. Helmut Schoen puts Germany ahead in the first half but Paddy Bradshaw's fourth goal in five internationals on 65 minutes guarantees a draw. Ireland will stay unbeaten until 1946. On September 3rd 1939, Great Britain declares war on Germany and international football virtually goes into hibernation. Of 30 matches played against a dozen different nations between making their debut in 1926 and the outbreak of war, Ireland had won 11 and lost 11.

THURSDAY 23RD MAY 2002

There's a showdown in Saipan as Mick McCarthy confronts Roy Keane over his comments about the Irish World Cup preparations that have been published in the *Irish Times*. Keane is furious at what he later describes in his autobiography as "unprofessionalism in the Irish camp". In a heated confrontation, Keane vents his spleen. "Mick, you're a liar... you're a f****** w*****," rages Keane to McCarthy in the squad's private dining room. "I didn't rate you as a player, I don't rate you as a manager, and I don't rate you as a person. You're a f***** w***** and you can stick your World Cup up your a***. The only reason I have any dealings with you is that somehow you are the manager of my country! You can stick it up your b*******."

SATURDAY 24TH MAY 1952

Ireland and Scotland draw 1-1 in an amateur international in Dublin.

TUESDAY 24TH MAY 1981

Packie Bonner makes his debut for Ireland on his 21st birthday and concedes two minutes into his first game as Andrzej Iwan scores for Poland. David O'Leary then puts one past Bonner before one of Ireland's greatest keepers concedes again on 66 minutes as the Poles win 3-0.

TUESDAY 24TH MAY 1994

Ireland planned on playing Portugal today but the Euro 96 qualifying draw pitted the two teams together and the Portuguese opt out. Jack Charlton is offered a list of replacement teams and opts for Bolivia, who prove tough opponents. The South Americans are going to the World Cup finals and John Sheridan's goal five minutes from time is the winner.

WEDNESDAY 25TH MAY 1966

The second and final game of a European tour takes Ireland to a rain-drenched Sclessin Stadium in Liege to play a strong Belgian team. Of the XI that started the previous fixture in Vienna, everyone retained their places despite a defeat apart from Frank O'Neill, who is replaced by Birmingham's Eric Barber. Ireland are twice behind but Noel Cantwell equalises on each occasion before Johnny Fullam bags a 3-2 win on 66 minutes. "The pity is that Eire failed to qualify for the World Cup," wrote Tom Muldowney in *World Soccer*. "On this showing, and with most of the team 'at home' in England, they could have shocked the best."

SUNDAY 25TH MAY 1986

Jack Charlton's relationship with David O'Leary takes a turn for the worse as the Irish central defender is left out of the team that starts the Iceland Triangular Tournament today with a game against the hosts. O'Leary's message that he could not make the last Irish game did not reach Charlton, who leaves him behind without explanation. Then, as Ireland's squad typically becomes depleted by injuries, Charlton phones O'Leary but he has booked a family holiday and refuses to change his plans. Despite the withdrawals, Ireland beat Iceland 2-1.

SATURDAY 25TH MAY 2002

"After Thursday's turbulent meeting in Saipan, as long as Mick McCarthy is in charge, I don't see Roy playing for Ireland again," reflects Niall Quinn in his *World Cup Diary* the day after Ireland's World Cup squad flies to Japan without Roy Keane. "It saddens me to see his international career finish like this – if it is finished." Away from the furore, Ireland beat club side Hiroshima 2-1 in front of 11,000 Irish fans.

TUESDAY 26TH MAY 1992

Ireland kick off their 1994 World Cup qualifying campaign with a fixture against Albania at Lansdowne Road. Due to being in a seven-team group, the match is played before the Euro 92 finals Ireland have failed to qualify for have even begun. Jack Charlton expects victory but the game is goalless at half-time until John Aldridge opens the scoring on 61 minutes and a second 10 minutes from time from Paul McGrath bags a 2-0 win. "Albania, for all their deficiencies, had fought the good fight and we were convinced that there would be no favours available to us on the road to the United States in 1994," wrote Charlton.

WEDNESDAY 26TH MAY 1993

Three months ago, Jack Charlton had visited Tirana – the Albanian capital that is the scene of Ireland's game today – to watch a World Cup qualifier with Northern Ireland, who were treated so shabbily by their hosts that Albania were slapped down by Fifa. "In all my years of football, I had seldom seen a visiting team given such shabby treatment, literally and otherwise, as that meted out to Billy Bingham and his players," said Charlton. On returning today, the toilet in his hotel room is still not working but everything else has improved, including the Albanian team who give Ireland a real workout on the pitch. After eight minutes, Suleyman Demollair hits a 30-yard pass to Sokel Kushta who slams the ball past Packie Bonner. The temperature has reached the high seventies but Roy Keane and Andy Townsend never slacken and Steve Staunton soon equalises from a free kick. The Albanians look like holding out for a draw that would damage Ireland's World Cup qualifying campaign until late substitute Tony Cascarino scores within minutes of coming on for John Aldridge to take all the points for Ireland.

THURSDAY 26TH MAY 1994

Jack Charlton is awarded the freedom of the city of Dublin and underestimates quite what it means. "I'd once been made an honorary Irishman by Charlie Haughey and that didn't create too much interest among the public," says Charlton, who is stunned to find a crowd of thousands of Dubliners on the streets when he arrives at College Green.

SUNDAY 26TH MAY 2002

Mick McCarthy flies by helicopter to Kobe to watch Ireland's first World Cup finals opponents Cameroon play England in a friendly but the fallout from his row with Roy Keane, who has left the Irish camp, continues. "I am not enjoying this World Cup experience," writes McCarthy today.

FRIDAY 26TH MAY 2006

Doctor Kevin Patrick O'Flanagan, one of Ireland's great sporting all-rounders, passes away aged 86. He made his debut for Bohemians aged just 16 and his first Ireland start two years later, when in November 1937 he features in a 3-3 draw with Norway in a World Cup qualifier at Dalymount Park. Playing inside-left, he scores. O'Flanagan also played rugby for University College Dublin and in 1942 featured for Ireland against the British Army at Ravenhill. He won all of his ten Irish caps at Bohemians, then moved to London in 1945 and signed for Arsenal. He continued playing rugby – for London Irish – and in 1947 played an unofficial test against France then gained a full cap in a 16-3 defeat to the touring Australians back at Lansdowne Road. An Irish sprint champion at 60 and 100 metres, he also excelled at the long-jump and would have gone to the Olympics if World War II had not intervened.

WEDNESDAY 26TH MAY 1976

Don Givens becomes Ireland's all-time top scorer after the Queens Park Rangers forward nets both goals in a 2-0 win in Poland.

TUESDAY 27TH MAY 1969

When Charlie Hurley arrived at the airport for Ireland's match in Copenhagen today, he thought he was travelling solely as a coach. Surprised to find he is expected to play, the Sunderland player admits he has not brought any boots. This is an early set back for Ireland in a game that must be won and would provide sobering debuts for Don Givens and Billy Newman. Givens was still in the youth team at Old Trafford and had yet to feature in the first XI. Eamon Dunphy also came back in with Johnny Giles surprisingly dropped. John Dempsey has to be rescued from a one-woman pitch invasion and two Ole Sorensen goals give Denmark a 2-0 triumph.

THURSDAY 27th MAY 1982

The Irish are only 1-0 down at half-time to a star-studded Brazilian team full of names like Falcao, Zico and Socrates but the second half in Uberlandia sees the heat take its toll. Jim McDonough lets in six second-half goals as Ireland fall to their biggest-ever international defeat, a 7-0 pasting. The manager today, Eoin Hand, is also in charge when Ireland secure their biggest win, 8-0 over Malta.

TUESDAY 27th MAY 1986

Ireland win their first trophy beating Czechoslovakia 1-0 in the Iceland Triangular Tournament in Reykjavik. After defeating the hosts two days earlier, a goal from Frank Stapleton seven minutes from time today is enough for a 1-0 win, making the final game between Iceland and the Czechs two days later meaningless. Jack Charlton gets to collect a trophy in only his fourth game in charge of the Irish team. "We have tightened up our game," says Frank Stapleton. "Our game may not be attractive to watch, but there is a new eagerness in the squad."

THURSDAY 27th MAY 2010

"We know with France, they have the ability to handball – we don't have that," says Robbie Keane, who, with the World Cup in South Africa coming up and Ireland absent, has clearly not forgiven Thierry Henry or the French nation for *that* handball.

WEDNESDAY 28th MAY 1924

The IFSFA struggled to raise funds to send a team to the 1924 Olympics for their international bow. Celtic came to Ireland to play a game against an IFSFA XI to raise money towards the £837 cost of sending a team to Paris but after deductions, the game raises just £200. The Irish Olympic Council foot the bill and send a team of footballers to Paris. As a result, today's first game against Bulgaria does not count as a full international in most records. In front of 1,659 fans at Stade de Colombes, Dinny Hannon leads out Ireland. A poor game is goalless at half-time but Ireland take control in the second half with a goal from Paddy Duncan of St James's Gate on 70 minutes, which is enough to advance to the quarter-finals.

SUNDAY 28TH MAY 1989

Ireland see off Malta 2-0 at Lansdowne Road with goals from Ray Houghton and Kevin Moran that brings World Cup qualification one step closer.

TUESDAY 28TH MAY 2002

By his own admission, it's one of the worst days of Mick McCarthy's life as on an overnight broadcast on RTÉ Roy Keane issues a mea culpa over his departure from the Irish World Cup camp. McCarthy is adamant that Keane cannot come back as he will lose face among the remaining players. "I am heading into a no-win situation," writes McCarthy, who is worried that he will have to quit after the finals are over. McCarthy says the door is still open to Keane but only if he receives a personal phone call.

TUESDAY 29TH MAY 1934

Mick Meagan, the first manager of the Irish football team to have a say in selection, is born in Dublin. A central defender for Everton and Huddersfield Town, Meagan wins 17 caps for Ireland between 1961 and 1969 then takes charge of the team for two years after retiring.

SUNDAY 29TH MAY 1994

Ireland play their penultimate friendly before embarking for next month's World Cup finals in the United States and travel to Hannover to play Germany. Jack Charlton felt a "nagging doubt that we might get a hiding" but goals from Tony Cascarino and Gary Kelly show Ireland are in great form.

WEDNESDAY 29TH MAY 2002

Roy Keane issues a statement saying that the Manchester United player will not be returning to the Irish camp for the World Cup after his fall-out with manager Mick McCarthy. "I do not consider that the best interests of Irish football will be served by my returning to the World Cup," says Keane. "The damage has been done." McCarthy later writes: "Keane clearly feels he has nothing to apologise for. He maintains that he was right and proper to speak to me the way he did, in front of my players and staff, last Thursday night."

WEDNESDAY 30TH MAY 1951

Johnny Carey wins his 25th cap for the Republic of Ireland in a 3-2 win away to Norway in Oslo and receives a Shamrock Statuette to mark the occasion. In the game, on 17 minutes Everton's Peter Farrell equalises an early Norwegian strike but the Norwegians regain the lead in the second half before Sheffield United outside-right Alf Ringstead levels on 67 minutes. With eight minutes before full time, Paddy Coad of Shamrock Rovers pops in the winner to the disappointment of the majority of the 20,900 crowd at the Ullevaal. Coad's goal is the first by a substitute for Ireland.

SUNDAY 30TH MAY 1971

Left-back Jimmy Holmes beats Steve Heighway's record and becomes the youngest Irish international after replacing Don Givens during a 4-1 defeat to Austria in a European Championship qualifier at Dalymount Park. Holmes is 17 years and 200 days old. He comes from Meath Square and initially played for Dublin side St John Bosco before moving to England and Coventry City in 1970. In March 1977, Spurs pay £120,000 for Holmes and he goes on to win 30 caps for Ireland.

THURSDAY 30TH MAY 2002

Fifa turn down the FAI's request to bring in Colin Healy as a last-minute replacement for Roy Keane, who has quit their World Cup finals squad.

FRIDAY 31ST MAY 2002

The Gaelic Athletic Association fax the FAI management and the Irish players in Saipan to wish them well ahead of tomorrow's opening World Cup finals match with Cameroon.

REPUBLIC OF IRELAND
On This Day

JUNE

WEDNESDAY 1st JUNE 1921

The Irish Free State Football Association – the organisation that will eventually become known as the FAI – is born today with a meeting at Molesworth Hall in Dublin. Plans are struck to play a League of Ireland featuring eight teams next season.

WEDNESDAY 1st JUNE 1977

Only five Irishmen have ever been sent off in an international and no-one has been sent off in two competitive matches. But, Mick Martin manages that feat today when he is sent packing – along with Noel Campbell – for a brawl eight minutes from the end of a 2-1 defeat to Bulgaria in Sofia. Campbell had only just come on the pitch as a substitute for Gerry Daly, making his sending off the quickest in Irish history and the first substitute to be dismissed for Ireland. Martin had also been shown the red card two years earlier during Ireland's 4-0 win over Turkey.

SATURDAY 1st JUNE 1991

Ireland take on the United States in a friendly watched by 51,000 fans at the Foxboro Stadium in Massachusetts. Tony Cascarino nets on 56 minutes for Ireland but Eric Wynalda ensures a 1-1 draw with an equaliser on 68 minutes. Irish manager Jack Charlton decides after the game that his players can have a night out. A decision that he later comes to regret…

SATURDAY 1st JUNE 2002

The Roy Keane–Mick McCarthy row has dominated Ireland's World Cup preparations but is forgotten today as the action moves to the pitch and the first group match with Cameroon. The game kicks off at 3.30pm local time but Fifa want the Irish team in the Niigata Stadium two hours before kick-off. Ireland start nervy and Shay Given is forced into an early save from Patrick Mboma. A young Samuel Eto'o is also causing problems and Mboma nets the opener. An injured Jason McAteer is substituted at half-time with Steve Finnan coming on. After 52 minutes, Matt Holland scores. Ireland finish the game the stronger team but cannot find a winner.

MONDAY 2ND JUNE 1924

Ireland are in the quarter-finals of the Olympics and face the Netherlands at Stade de Colombes. An Irish side, including five players from Athlone Town, find themselves a goal down in minutes. Frank Ghent, the only fresh face from the Irish side that beat Bulgaria in the first round, equalises on 32 minutes. The game goes to extra time during which Fermenoy adds a second from a soft free kick to settle the tie. The two sides are staying close to each other and go for a meal together afterwards. That evening, Ireland agree to take on Estonia, who have also been eliminated, in a friendly before going home.

THURSDAY 2ND JUNE 1949

Ireland face 1948 Olympic champions Sweden in a World Cup qualifier. All but Tommy Godwin and Liam Coad of the Irish XI play in Britain. Davy Walsh of West Bromwich Albion puts the visitors ahead at Stockholm's rainy Rasunda Stadium, netting a poor clearance from a tight angle. Sweden sweep forward and are 2-1 up by the break, Nils Liedholm completing a 3-1 win with a second-half header.

SUNDAY 2ND JUNE 1957

The mother of Mark Lawrenson, who was born today in Preston, wanted her son to be Jesuit priest. Instead, he became one of Ireland's most stylish defenders. He attended a Jesuit school but joined Preston North End then moved to Brighton & Hove Albion where he made more than 150 appearances and broke into the Ireland team. In 1981, Liverpool paid a then club-record fee of £900,000 for Lawrenson. He won the First Division title and the 1984 European Cup with Liverpool, and 39 caps for Ireland, before his Achilles tendon snapped, ending his career.

SUNDAY 2ND JUNE 1991

Having enjoyed a night out, Jack Charlton's Ireland team touring the US are due to meet in the hotel at 7.30am this morning. Everyone is there but a young Roy Keane. "Nineteen years old, your first trip, do you have any idea how long we have been waiting?" rages Charlton at Keane, when he appears 30 minutes later. "I didn't ask you to wait, did I?" replies the fearless Keane.

SATURDAY 2ND JUNE 1999

Unbeaten in their first six World Cup qualifiers, Ireland host Portugal. Clinton Morrison is able to make his international bow after the Crystal Palace player, with an Irish grandmother, gets clearance. Portugal are without captain Fernando Couto, suspended by Fifa over nandrolone offences. Their association claim the FAI colluded with Fifa to put Couto out of the match and when the Portuguese arrive in Dublin their president complains he should be picked up in a BMW or Mercedes not the FAI Opel. Manager Antonio Oliveira snubs Mick McCarthy and Ireland are charged up. The wind is not conducive to a good game but Roy Keane controls a Stephen Carr throw and hits home on 68 minutes only for Luis Figo to guarantee a share of the points with a goal ten minutes later. After the game, Oliveira refuses to shake McCarthy's hand and a confrontation ensues.

SUNDAY 2ND JUNE 2002

Family day for the Irish World Cup team in Japan, 24 hours after their opening game with Cameroon, as the players meet with wives, girlfriends and children.

SATURDAY 3RD JUNE 1995

The nadir of Jack Charlton's reign as Irish manager as his team are held to a 0-0 draw by Liechtenstein in a Euro 96 qualifier in Vaduz. Ireland had won the home leg 4-0. When Niall Quinn goes close early on, the large contingent of Irish fans in the 4,500 crowd expect another whipping but despite having 37 chances, according to one newspaper, Charlton's side cannot find a way past the woodwork or home keeper Martin Heeb. "Ireland drew 0-0 with a mountaintop," wrote Peter Ball of the *Irish Independent*.

TUESDAY 4TH JUNE 1924

Two days after being eliminated from the Olympic football tournament, Ireland are still in Paris and play Estonia in a friendly. Goals from Paddy Duncan, Christy Robinson of Bohemians, and Frank Ghent of Athlone Town, produce a 3-1 win. Before departing home for Ireland, the Irish agree to play a fixture with the United States, but the cost of going to the Olympics again weighs heavy and Ireland do not return for 24 years.

SUNDAY 4TH JUNE 1989

Hungary visit Dublin for the 250th international at Lansdowne Road. The winners will go to the World Cup finals in Italy and Hungary come closest to scoring early on, Packie Bonner making a fine save from Laszlo Distzl. Ireland then begin to threaten and when Steve Staunton's cross is headed off the Hungarian line, Paul McGrath volleys home. Ireland revert to 4-5-1 as Liam Brady comes on as a substitute for John Aldridge. Hungary camp in the Irish half but Bonner will not be beaten and ten minutes from time Tony Cascarino gets Ireland's second.

THURSDAY 4TH JUNE 1992

Packie Bonner becomes the first goalkeeper to be sent off for Ireland, when he is dismissed after 63 minutes during a 2-0 defeat to Italy in the US Cup at the Foxboro Stadium.

SUNDAY 4TH JUNE 2000

Ireland take on Mexico in the US Cup at Soldier Field in Chicago. Mexico are weakened by club calls but there is no revenge for a 1994 World Cup defeat for the Irish, who are missing Roy Keane through injury. Mick McCarthy tries a 4-3-3 system but two wide men supporting Robbie Keane is, in his own words, a "big mistake". Mexico surge into a two-goal lead that could have been worse but for the brilliance of Dean Kiely; Ireland rally and Richard Dunne and Dominic Foley goals produce a 2-2 draw.

WEDNESDAY 5TH JUNE 1965

The Irish were written off ahead of this World Cup qualifier with Spain. Three Manchester United players are in the Irish starting XI; Pat and Tony Dunne, and Shay Brennan, who becomes the first Englishman to represent Ireland after Fifa change their rules to allow a player not wanted by the land of their birth to play for the land of their parents. Brennan is magnificent. After Jose Cortajarena puts through his own net on 61 minutes, Ireland refuse to surrender, hanging on for a famous 1-0 win. "An unpleasant shock to the knowing ones who wrote off the Irish as soon as the draw was announced," wrote Tom Muldowney in *World Soccer*.

SUNDAY 5TH JUNE 1994

Ireland play their final match before departing for the US and the World Cup finals against the Czech Republic. Nearly 44,000 fans cram into Lansdowne Road as Jack Charlton tries to produce a spectacle by giving John Sheridan and Andy Townsend greater freedom in midfield. Against a team that two years later would reach the final of Euro 96, Ireland are torn apart by the promptings of Martin Frydek. Andy Townsend equalises just before half-time, after the Czechs had earlier taken the lead, but the visitors score twice in the second half to leave Irish fans uneasy about their chances in America.

WEDNESDAY 5TH JUNE 2002

Ireland must not lose to Germany at the World Cup today but look like doing just that after Miroslav Klose scores for the Germans in their vital World Cup group match at the Kashima Stadium in Japan. Before the game, Steve Staunton is presented with a Cartier watch to mark 14 years with Ireland. In the Kashima Soccer Stadium at Ibaraki, Ireland press but luck is with the Germans. With the match virtually over, Robbie Keane sends the Irish fans delirious as he delivers Niall Quinn's header into the German net. "I think it's beyond question that we deserved the draw," wrote Quinn afterwards. "Oliver Kahn was by far the busier goalkeeper. In fact, he showed just how good he is – world-class in my opinion. And he needed to be to make those saves, particularly the one from Damien Duff."

WEDNESDAY 6TH JUNE 1973

Sean Thomas had one match in charge of Ireland. That was today when the Bohemians manager led the Irish to Oslo for a friendly with Norway. Miah Dennehy of Cork Hibernians put Ireland ahead on 17 minutes but Hans Paulsen equalised in the second half, leaving Thomas with an international record of played one, drawn one.

MONDAY 6TH JUNE 1994

Thousands of Irish fans congregate as Ireland board an Aer Lingus flight out of Dublin for America and the World Cup finals. Charlton and a handful of the FAI officials get upgraded to first class; the players sit at the rear.

TUESDAY 6TH JUNE 2000

Constant rain at the Foxboro Stadium in Boston mars Ireland's US Cup match with the United States. "Anywhere else and I don't think the match would have been played, so heavy was the downpour," writes Irish manager Mick McCarthy. Dominic Foley manages to put Ireland ahead on 31 minutes but a goal from Ante Razov, who looked clearly offside, rescues a draw for the hosts.

WEDNESDAY 6TH JUNE 2001

After the highly-charged previous home game with Portugal four days earlier, Ireland fly to Tallinn for another World Cup qualifier and two first-half goals from Richard Dunne and Matt Holland are enough for a 2-0 win and all the points. A home win in their next game against Holland and Ireland are guaranteed a play-off spot at least.

FRIDAY 7TH JUNE 2002

There are a few sore heads among the Irish players and management this morning after a late night. "Some proponents of the modern game will frown at alcohol intake in the middle of a World Cup," writes manager Mick McCarthy in his diary today. "Some will slam it as traditionalist, a relic from a bygone age. Rubbish. There were no question marks raised against my players in the 92nd minute of the game against Germany. They deserve to let their hair down after a big game."

SUNDAY 8TH JUNE 1969

Ireland's World Cup qualifying campaign started with two defeats and Hungary make that three today. Charlie Hurley's international playing days are nearly over and he did not even bring his boots to the last game. Today provides Ireland's player-coach with his international swansong. Although Don Givens scores his first goal for Ireland in only his second start, a Bene goal ten minutes from time clinches a 2-1 success for Hungary.

TUESDAY 8TH JUNE 1971

Johnny Carey is sacked as manager of Blackburn Rovers along with his assistant Eddie Quigley. The former Ireland team manager was in his second spell at Rovers but never managed again after today.

TUESDAY 9TH JUNE 1992

Ireland's games in the US Cup finished two days ago and manager Jack Charlton is having regrets. "The choice was to give the lads an extra fortnight's holiday, or alternatively, to take them on tour," wrote Charlton today. "I decided to leave the decision to the players and they opted for a tour. At that point they were up to their necks in cup and championship football in Britain, and the prospect of a nice leisurely tour seemed very attractive. It was a judgement which they, like me, would later question very seriously."

WEDNESDAY 9TH JUNE 1993

Eight games into their World Cup qualifying campaign and Ireland are unbeaten as they take on Latvia in Riga. Paul McGrath missed the last game through injury and upset Jack Charlton by failing to convey the news personally. McGrath soon calls up to apologise and is back in the side today. To complete his apology, he scores Ireland's second goal two minutes from half-time that – coupled with John Aldridge's goal on 15 minutes – is enough for a 2-0 win. Aldridge's goal is the 400th scored by Ireland in international football.

FRIDAY 10TH JUNE 1988

The European Championships begin today with a game between the hosts West Germany and Italy. Ireland kick off two days later and manager Jack Charlton has a plan. "I know the way I don't want them to play, but I also know the way I want them to play," says Charlton in Germany. "I think they might play the way I want them to play if I don't say too much."

FRIDAY 10TH JUNE 1994

Ireland's World Cup squad arrived in the US resort of Orlando three days ago to train for the World Cup finals and endure three days of rain until today, when the sun finally comes out, making training easier.

MONDAY 10TH JUNE 2002

Niall Quinn wins 14,000 Yen from his Irish World Cup teammates after donning goalkeeper's gloves for a penalty-training session.

MONDAY 11TH JUNE 1990

Ireland's first-ever match in a World Cup finals. The Irish have been paired in a group with the Netherlands, Egypt and England. Jack Charlton gets to start his campaign in a meeting with fellow England international Bobby Robson as the Irish take on England in the Sardinian city of Cagliari. England are playing against a strong wind but manage to get ahead after Packie Bonner is lured off his goal-line by a Chris Waddle cross. Gary Lineker is being pursued by Irish captain Mick McCarthy and Chris Houghton but the England striker manages to chest the ball over the Irish line. McCarthy later admits responsibility but England are unable to build on their lead. After an electrical storm at half-time, Charlton brings on Alan McLoughlin to press from midfield. Bobby Robson introduces Steve McMahon for the same reason but the Liverpool player fumbles a ball that falls to Kevin Sheedy, who drives home an equaliser.

TUESDAY 11TH JUNE 2002

The Irish take on Saudi Arabia in the final group match at the World Cup finals and, after drawing with Cameroon and Germany in their previous matches, need a two-goal win today. After breakfast in Chiba, the Irish players travel to the International Stadium in Yokohama for their show-down. "What if the Saudis score?" frets manager Mick McCarthy. "What if we just get one goal?" He need not have worried about scoring. Robbie Keane finds the net after seven minutes but the wait for a second goal goes on until the 61st minute, when Gary Breen slams a Steve Staunton through-ball past Mohammed Al-Deayea. With three minutes left, Damien Duff confirms Ireland's passage and a 3-0 win.

SUNDAY 11TH JUNE 2006

Ireland's US Cup campaign comes to an end with a fixture at the Giants Stadium in New York against South Africa, who score first through Benni McCarthy but cannot protect their lead. Strikes from Stephen McPhail and Niall Quinn bag the points but the title goes to the hosts, who beat Mexico in the day's other game. After being put up out-of-town in Chicago and Boston for their two previous US Cup fixtures, the players enjoy a night in Manhattan, taking in Fitzpatrick's bar.

SUNDAY 12TH JUNE 1988

Ireland play their first-ever match in a major international finals and their English manager Jack Charlton comes up against the team he won the World Cup with 22 years ago. The English confidently believe they are favourites but Charlton believes otherwise. "They may be joint favourites in England, but I'm not sure they are joint favourites in Europe – unless Ladbrokes have opened up over there." After just five minutes of the match at the Neckar Stadium in Stuttgart, Ray Houghton sends the Irish fans into raptures by scoring. Ireland do not play well but poor English finishing, and an inspired Packie Bonner, keep England out and the Irish win 1-0.

WEDNESDAY 12TH JUNE 2002

The FAI start talking to Ireland manager Mick McCarthy about a new six-year contract.

MONDAY 12TH JUNE 2006

Roy Keane announces his retirement from professional football.

MONDAY 13TH JUNE 1994

Weekend media coverage of Ireland's World Cup preparations has left Jack Charlton seething. Three days earlier, the Irish manager said that his players could have the odd beer providing it was authorised and controlled. The response from their own media and the London press, who have no British teams to cover, produces headlines like 'Carry on Boozing Says Jack' that leaves the former England international raging. "Bloody crap," Charlton writes in his World Cup Diary today. "I never said any such thing."

SATURDAY 14TH JUNE 1924

The Free State play their first game in Dublin. While at the Olympic football tournament in Paris, Ireland arranged a friendly with the United States and 5,000 turn up at Dalymount Park today. Eight of Ireland's XI had played in Paris but Ned Brooks was not one of them. He missed Ireland's Olympic debut because of work commitments but makes up for that today as the Bohemians player scores a hat-trick to see Ireland home 3-1.

TUESDAY 14TH JUNE 1994

Ireland play the United States under-21 team in a final run-out before opening their World Cup programme in four days time and win 4-2 with David Kelly getting two of the goals.

SUNDAY 15TH JUNE 1986

After a dream start to their European Championship finals debut, Ireland face the Soviet Union in Hannover. The 45,290 crowd is flooded with Irish supporters, who witness one of the most spectacular goals of Jack Charlton's era as Ronnie Whelan bicycle-kicks a huge Mick McCarthy throw past a stunned Rinat Dasaev, the Soviet captain and goalkeeper. In their best performance of the tournament, Ireland have numerous other chances to score but allow Oleg Protasov to equalise for the eventual runners-up 15 minutes from time.

WEDNESDAY 15TH JUNE 1994

Jack Charlton's relationship with the media at the World Cup finals in America is rapidly deteriorating. After falling out with the print media over what he felt were disingenuous headlines at the weekend, Charlton turns on the television companies today. During his argument with the print media, Charlton was unwittingly being filmed by TV cameras that he thought were switched off. The coverage makes for lively viewing. With Sky Sports declining to join the BBC, ITV, RTÉ and UTV in signing a contract that saw co-operation in return for payment, Charlton decrees that the cameras must be turned off when a press conference starts.

SUNDAY 16TH JUNE 1946

The FAI always eschewed selecting players from the north but for their first games after World War II, Billy McMillan and Jackie Vernon of Belfast Celtic, Arsenal's Josiah Sloan, and Jimmy McAlinden of Portsmouth, are named in the squad for a brief European tour that starts in Portugal. No reason is given for the volte face. A fifth Northern Ireland player, Davy Cochrane of Shamrock Rovers, was also selected but decided not to go due to being afraid of flying. In Lisbon, Peter Farrell is made captain on his debut but Ireland are downed 3-1 in front of a 60,000 crowd. Jack O'Reilly is the scorer.

WEDNESDAY 16TH JUNE 1993

A second game in the Baltic inside a week and Ireland want another win after their success in Latvia as qualifying for next year's World Cup finals in the United States reaches its climax. Ireland have never won three times in a row away from home and a crowd of 6,000 in Vilnius see a tight match. When Roy Keane is fouled outside the box, Steve Staunton hammers in a free kick on 38 minutes that deflects off the heel of the host's best player, Baltusnikas, for the only goal of the game. "Now America beckons," wrote Jack Charlton. "Barring a catastrophe, I am pretty certain that these three wins will qualify us for the finals."

SUNDAY 16TH JUNE 2002

Ireland have left Japan and flown to Suwon in South Korea to face Spain in the last 16 of the World Cup. "I think that the days of Ireland just being happy to qualify for a tournament are over," writes Niall Quinn in his *World Cup Diary*. "We are going to have far more serious intentions from now on." Can they beat the Spanish? When Fernando Morientes scores after a long throw from Carles Puyol just eight minutes into the game, this seems unlikely but Ireland never give up. The game is virtually over when Swedish referee Anders Frisk notices Hierro pulling on Niall Quinn's shirt. Frisk points to the penalty spot, Keane converts and the game goes into extra time, then penalties, but Spain prevail 3-2.

SUNDAY 17TH JUNE 1990

A win today for Ireland over Egypt will take the Irish through to the second round of the World Cup finals on their first appearance at this stage. Jack Charlton stuck with the same XI that had started against England in their last match. Ronnie Whelan is again on the bench. Ireland's tactic is to close down their opponents' space but this is just what the North Africans come to do. Egypt could also qualify and rarely pass the halfway line that, combined with North African time-wasting, produces a wretched match. The 0-0 scoreline provides yet more fuel for Eamon Dunphy's regular criticism of Charlton in the *Sunday Independent*.

RAY HOUGHTON CELEBRATES HIS EARLY GOAL AGAINST ITALY ON 18TH JUNE 1994, WHICH WAS ENOUGH TO GIVE IRELAND A 1-0 WIN OVER ITALY IN NEW YORK IN THE 1994 WORLD CUP.

THURSDAY 17TH JUNE 1999

Uefa fine the FAI around £25,000 after a Euro 2000 qualifier scheduled for Dublin earlier in the month has to be abandoned, when the Irish government refuse to grant visas to the visiting Yugoslavian players.

SATURDAY 18TH JUNE 1988

The Netherlands stand between Ireland and a place in the semi-finals of the European Championship. "Pressure?" reflects Dutch manager Rinus Michels. "We all feel pressure, everyone is human – even the Irish." In front of a massive 70,800 crowd at Gelsenkirchen, a draw would put Ireland into the semi-finals. The Irish barely get out of their own half but look to have held on for a third successive draw until eight minutes from time, Wim Kieft breaks Irish hearts and hands the Dutch a 1-0 win. A week later, Ruud Gullit lifts the trophy for Holland.

SATURDAY 18TH JUNE 1994

Ireland play Italy in their opening World Cup finals match but Jack Charlton's day starts badly after an Indian journalist rings his hotel room at four o'clock in the morning to ask for his team line-up. At the Giants Stadium in New York, 77,000 fans create what Charlton calls an "awe-inspiring" sight. The Irish fans out-sing the Italian supporters during the national anthems. After 12 minutes, Ray Houghton volleys a woeful Franco Baresi clearance straight past Gianluca Pagliuca. The Irish management and many fans fear Ireland scored too early; many begin to accept a draw. But Italy do not score. Roberto Baggio is denied by a fine reflex save from Packie Bonner, and a good Denis Irwin tackle, but Ireland are rarely threatened as their campaign gets off to the best possible start.

SUNDAY 19TH JUNE 1994

Jack Charlton travels to Washington to watch Mexico, Ireland's next opponents in the World Cup finals, take on Norway – and wishes he hasn't. Charlton's flight is delayed, he has a row with Fifa officials who refuse to give water bags to the players in stifling heat, then electrical storms stop all flights back to Ireland's training base in Orlando. Charlton spends the night on a hard plastic seat in the airport.

WEDNESDAY 20TH JUNE 1956

Mike Walsh is born in Manchester. He starts out with Bolton Wanderers, where he is captain. In 1981 he signs for Howard Kendall at Everton and makes his only four Irish appearances the next year.

THURSDAY 21ST JUNE 1990

After two draws in two World Cup games, Ireland must avoid defeat today against the Dutch, one of only two teams to have beaten the Irish in a competitive international over the last two years. All the games in the group, also including England and Egypt, have been draws. Ruud Gullit scores after 10 minutes in Palermo and Ireland look in trouble against the European champions. After an hour, Jack Charlton brings on Tony Cascarino and Ronnie Whelan but the breakthrough is provided by Packie Bonner's huge punt upfield. The keeper's clearance bounces awkwardly in the Dutch penalty area and Niall Quinn scores for a 1-1 draw. With England beating Egypt, Ireland finished group runners-up having scored more goals than Holland.

TUESDAY 22ND JUNE 2010

A 38th-minute free kick from Megan Campbell is enough for Ireland's under-17 girls team to upset reigning champions Germany in the semi-final of the Uefa Championships at Nyon in Switzerland. Noel King's team created a sensation by qualifying unbeaten in a run that included a 2-1 win over Sweden, one of the superpowers of European football, in a previous qualifying round in April.

SUNDAY 23RD JUNE 1946

In only their second game after the end of World War II, Ireland beat Spain 1-0 in front of a 35,000 crowd at Madrid's Metropolitano Stadium. Joe Sloan scores the only goal of the game in the first half, knocking home a Jack O'Reilly pass.

THURSDAY 23RD JUNE 1948

The Irish team to play at the 1948 Olympic Games in London is chosen. Manchester United and Ireland star Johnny Carey will coach the side, whose players must all be amateur. The side is drawn exclusively from the LOI with Bohemians providing five players – more than any other club.

FRIDAY 24TH JUNE 1994

The temperature at Orlando's Citrus Bowl Stadium in Orlando, where Ireland take on Mexico in their second World Cup finals game, is 110 degrees. For the first half hour, Ireland nearly take the lead but Tommy Coyne just fails to connect with a cross. Denis Irwin gets a harsh yellow card for taking his time in the oppressive heat, which suits Mexico much better and the Central Americans take a two-goal lead with strikes either side of half-time by Luis Postigo. The linesman refuses to allow water bags on the pitch. Jack Charlton complains to the fourth Fifa match official and water is distributed. Then he has another row as his attempt to bring on substitute John Aldridge is ignored. Aldridge eventually comes on and scores six minutes from time but Mexico win.

SUNDAY 25TH JUNE 1972

Mick Leech of Shamrock Rovers scores Ireland's 250th international goal but his side go down 2-1 to Portugal at Recife in the final game of the Brazil Independence Cup. Ireland started brightly last week, beating Ecuador 3-2 but went down 2-1 to Chile four days ago and finish third.

MONDAY 25TH JUNE 1990

Genoa: Ireland are on the verge of the World Cup quarter-finals. Many of the players in the team for opponents Romania won the 1986 European Cup with Steaua Bucharest. Gheorge Hagi is at the centre of the best moves for either team and twice the Romanian brings fine saves from Packie Bonner. At the other end, Kevin Sheedy presses Sliviu Lung into service but no-one could score. After extra time comes the agony of penalties. David O'Leary had only taken one penalty for club side Arsenal but strides up for the vital kick: 5-4 to Ireland.

SATURDAY 25TH JUNE 1994

Jack Charlton returns to his Florida hotel to find out from the media he has been fined 20,000 Swiss francs and banned from the bench for one game by Fifa for arguing with match officials over his attempt to bring on John Aldridge during the previous day's game with Mexico. Aldridge is fined for swearing at an official.

THE IRISH GIRLS' UNDER-17 TEAM CELEBRATE THEIR VICTORY OVER REIGNING CHAMPIONS GERMANY IN THE SEMI-FINALS OF THE UEFA EUROPEAN CHAMPIONSHIPS IN JUNE 2010.

SATURDAY 26TH JUNE 2010

Noel King's Irish girls' under-17 team face Spain in the final of the Uefa Championships in Nyon but go down 4-1 in a penalty shoot-out after the game ended scoreless.

MONDAY 27TH JUNE 1994

A collection in Irish pubs raises £10,000 to pay Jack Charlton's fine. Charlton insists he will pay the fine himself and that the money is donated to charity.

MONDAY 28TH JUNE 1971

Kenneth Edward Cunningham, better known as Kenny, is born in Dublin. After starting out at Tolka Rovers, he moves to England and Millwall in 1988 and spends six years with the club, making more than 130 appearances before joining Wimbledon, where, two years after signing, he finally breaks into the Ireland team in 1996. A defender, over the next decade, Cunningham wins 70 caps for Ireland, later playing for Birmingham City and Sunderland before retiring after the Irish miss out on the 2006 World Cup finals.

TUESDAY 28TH JUNE 1994

All four teams in World Cup Group E are locked on three points apiece. Ireland really need to beat Norway to be sure of making the last 16 of the finals in America and return to the scene of their opening-day triumph, Giants Stadium in New York. After a nightmare in the Mexican game, Paul McGrath is pleasantly surprised to find he has retained his place but John Aldridge comes into the starting XI in place of Tommy Coyne. Jack Charlton is serving a one-match ban and watches the game from a TV commentary position, leaving assistant Maurice Setters to look after matters pitchside. A tight game in front of more than 76,000 fans sees few chances. With a quarter of an hour to go, Ronnie Whelan and David Kelly come on as substitutes and the former nearly nets a winner but is beaten to the ball by Norwegian keeper, Erik Thorstvedt. The game finishes goalless but with the other group fixture between Italy and Mexico finishing 1-1, Ireland finish second and qualify for the next round.

WEDNESDAY 29TH JUNE 1994

Ireland's players have a free day at the World Cup after yesterday's decisive match but Jack Charlton jets off to Washington from Newark to catch Belgium against Saudi Arabia, who could – depending on results – be their next opponents in the last 16. The trip is wasted as the Netherlands will face Ireland and not for the first time during the competition, Charlton wishes he had stayed put. More electrical storms mean that flights from Washington back to the Irish camp in Orlando have been cancelled. Charlton gets a small flight to Atlanta in the hope of catching a connection to Orlando, but to no avail. He spends another night on a plastic chair in an airport lounge, this time in Atlanta.

SATURDAY 30TH JUNE 1990

Ireland made the quarter-finals of the Olympic football tournament on their debut 66 years earlier and emulate that achievement, albeit through a far lengthier route, in their first appearance in a World Cup finals. Today, Ireland play hosts Italy in Rome's Olympic Stadium for a place in the semi-finals of the World Cup. For half an hour, Ireland pressure Italy relentlessly, looking a much better team than during the dreary earlier draws with England and Egypt. Ireland even had the first two chances, headers from Paul McGrath and Niall Quinn, but would not threaten Walter Zenga's goal again. Baggio has an effort ruled out before Toto Schillaci scores on 37 minutes. Ireland press forward but Packie Bonner is the busier keeper as Ireland slide gallantly out.

REPUBLIC OF IRELAND
On This Day

JULY

FRIDAY 1st JULY 1994

Ireland hold their last training session before the game against the Netherlands in three days' time in an attempt to book a place in the quarter-finals of the World Cup for the second tournament in a row.

WEDNESDAY 2nd JULY 1997

The Irish under-20 team lose to Argentina in the semi-finals of the World under-20 championships at Kuching in Malaysia. Brian Kerr's team had qualified out of a group including Ghana, the USA and China for the last 16, where extra time was needed to beat Morocco 2-1. In the quarter-finals, the Irish upset Spain 1-0 but the run ends today.

FRIDAY 3rd JULY 2009

The chances of injury-hit Ireland star Stephen Reid playing in the national team's crucial World Cup qualifiers this autumn have improved, his club side Blackburn Rovers report today.

MONDAY 4th JULY 1994

Can Ireland reach the last eight of the World Cup again? The 1988 European champions are their opponents in the Citrus Bowl and Jack Charlton has left out Denis Irwin in favour of Gary Kelly – one of his hardest decisions during his time as Irish manager. Ireland beat Holland 1-0 in Tilburg three months earlier and if that result can be repeated the Irish will face hosts the United States or Brazil in Dallas. Within the first five minutes, Ireland almost score but Steve Staunton's powerful free kick is deflected and on 11 minutes Dennis Bergkamp puts the Dutch ahead. A Terry Phelan header does not reach Packie Bonner, allowing a Dutch player to intercept and Bergkamp side-foots in at the near post. Ireland fight back but Bonner cannot hold a Wim Jonk shot from 35 yards out, producing what Charlton describes as "the silliest goal I've seen in a long time". There is no way back. The Dutch go to Dallas, Ireland go home.

SATURDAY 5th JULY 1997

Ireland finish third in the Fifa under-20 World Championships in Malaysia after beating Ghana 2-1 in the play-off.

TUESDAY 6TH JULY 1976

Long before Rory Delap became synonymous with his punishing long throws for Stoke City, he was an Irish international. Born today in Sutton Coldfield, he plays in defence, midfield and up front for Carlisle United and in February 1998 Derby County snap him up for £500,000. He wins his first Irish cap in 1998 in a 2-1 defeat to the Czech Republic and later plays for Southampton and Sunderland before moving to the Potteries. Delap missed out on a place in the 2002 World Cup finals squad. With a record marked by withdrawals due to injury, the last of his 11 caps was in 2004.

FRIDAY 7TH JULY 2000

Mick Cooke resigns as manager of the Irish women's set-up after eight years to focus on his assistant manager's job at Shamrock Rovers. Under Cooke, the under-17 side won the Gothia Cup in 1995, the under-18s won the Dana Cup in 1996 and the seniors reached the European Championship third round.

TUESDAY 8TH JULY 1980

Born today in Tallaght, Robbie Keane's career began with his Football League debut for Wolverhampton Wanderers on the opening day of the 1997/98 season. Keane was just 17. On his first Irish start next year against the Czech Republic, he is the second youngest player to win a full cap. Keane switches club to Coventry City in 1999 then has a brief, ill-fated spell with Inter Milan, where Keane only makes six appearances. He returns to England and Leeds United, then switches to Spurs in 2002. Over the next six years for Spurs, he scores 80 goals in 197 appearances and collects the 1998 League Cup, before being sold for £19 million to Liverpool. After a year he returns to Spurs, then in 2009 is loaned to Glasgow Celtic. He won the under-16 and under-18 European Championships with Ireland under Brian Kerr and was part of the Irish team that reached the last 16 of the under-20 World Cup in 1999. Keane scores three goals in Ireland's four games at the 2002 World Cup finals and is appointed as national team captain by Steve Staunton, retaining this role under his replacement Giovanni Trapattoni. He averages a goal every other game for Ireland and is his country's all-time top scorer.

TUESDAY 9TH JULY 1974

Gary Kelly, who was born today in Drogheda, is a rarity among modern footballers as he spent his entire 16-year club career with Leeds United. He enjoyed the peaks of success, such as reaching the semi-finals of the Champions League, before retiring in 2007, aged just 32, as the club spiral downwards. He made his international debut in 1994 in a 0-0 draw with Russia and goes on to win 50 more caps up to 2003. The youngest of a family of 13, Kelly is the uncle of Ian Harte and the pair were both in the squad for the 2002 World Cup finals.

TUESDAY 10TH JULY 1956

When Frank Stapleton finally hung up his boots for Ireland after playing in the 1990 World Cup finals, he had racked up 71 appearances and was his country's top scorer with 20 goals. Stapleton, who was born today in Dublin, made the bulk of more than 600 Football League appearances with his first two clubs. He joined Arsenal in 1974, spent seven years at Highbury, then left in 1981 for Manchester United for £900,000 – a fee set by a tribunal because the clubs could not come to an agreement. After arriving at Old Trafford, he won the FA Cup for a second time in 1983 and 1985, becoming the first player to score in the final for two different winning teams. Stapleton's international debut was against Turkey in 1976 and he scores in a 3-3 draw in Istanbul but does not find the net again for Ireland until May 1978 and another 3-3 draw, this time in Copenhagen with Denmark. He plays in Euro 88 and the 1990 World Cup then moves into coaching.

WEDNESDAY 11TH JULY 1984

Coventry City give Luton Town Irish utility player Ashley Grimes and £100,000 for their full-back Kirk Stephens.

THURSDAY 12TH JULY 1956

Tony Galvin, who celebrates his birthday today, gave up on dreams of becoming a professional footballer to study for a Russian Studies degree at Hull University. He turned out for the university then Goole Town after graduating before Spurs swooped, paying a bargain £30,000 for a left-winger who would make more than 200 appearances for the club and win 29 caps for Ireland.

THURSDAY 13TH JULY 1911

Bill Gorman was only Irish by accident. His Scottish father and English mother were on holiday in Sligo when he was born today. Turning out in Scottish junior football for Shettleston, he made his Irish debut in a 1-0 win over Switzerland in 1936 but only won 13 caps as World War II interrupted his career. He later played for Bury and Brentford and his last cap was in a 2-0 defeat to Portugal in 1947.

THURSDAY 14TH JULY 1966

Better known now as a manager, Owen Columba Coyle won a solitary cap for Ireland, when he replaced Tommy Coyne for the last few minutes of a famous 1-0 Irish win in the Netherlands in April 1994. Unable to oust the settled Irish strike-force of John Aldridge, Tony Cascarino and Coyne, he never played again but proved a popular player for a range for Scottish clubs and Bolton Wanderers.

TUESDAY 15TH JULY 1958

A Londoner, Austin Hayes, was playing for Southampton when he was reportedly surprised to be called up by Ireland for their under-21 team by virtue of his ancestors. Hayes, who was born today, won a solitary full cap in a 1979 European Championship qualifier against Denmark. He was substituted in the second half by Johnny Giles and never featured again. Hayes had a sporadic club career that took in the Los Angeles Aztecs and Millwall. Tragically, he was diagnosed with lung cancer and died in December 1986, aged just 28.

TUESDAY 16TH JULY 2002

After selling exclusive rights to internationals to BSkyB, controlled by media baron Rupert Murdoch, the FAI are accused of selling the sport short. BSkyB paid the FAI €7.5m for four home internationals, four under-21 matches, two FAI Cup semi-finals and the FAI Cup final every year until 2006. In contrast, Sky is paying €500,000 a game over the same period to England's Football League to broadcast live matches from the Nationwide League and some Worthington Cup ties. A new supporters' group, Ireland Fans United, claims that the FAI has been "short-changed by Rupert Murdoch".

TUESDAY 17TH JULY 1928

Born today, Christy Giles' one Ireland cap was against Norway at Dalymount Park in November 1950. Down 2-0 after 11 minutes, Ireland rally for a 2-2 draw but Giles never features again. A Dubliner and outside-right, Giles began his club career with Drumcondra and won the LOI title in this first season with the Drums in 1947/48. Two years later, he is signed by Doncaster Rovers, where he is playing on his sole Irish appearance. Giles falls out with Doncaster after missing a league fixture with Coventry City to visit his sick wife despite the club denying him permission to go. He returned to the side but left in August 1953 for Aldershot, later playing for Portadown and Distillery in the Irish League.

FRIDAY 18TH JULY 1980

Liam Brady rejects a chance to sign for Manchester United after the Old Trafford club had offered Arsenal more than £1.5 million for his services.

TUESDAY 19TH JULY 1983

Ireland are drawn to play Northern Ireland in today's draw for the preliminary round of the Uefa youth championships.

WEDNESDAY 20TH JULY 1977

Johnny Giles has had plenty of job offers after deciding to leave his post as West Bromwich Albion manager but surprisingly buys half of Shamrock Rovers and appoints himself player-manager. "I would not exchange a little portion of Irish football or Irish life for all the lucrative offers that have been publicised," he tells *The Times*.

THURSDAY 20TH JULY 2000

Former FAI president Charlie Walsh passes away at his home in Drogheda. He was president from 1974 to 1976 but his longest post with the FAI was treasurer during the heady days of the 1980s and 1990s and he was in that role on his retirement in 1994.

FRIDAY 21ST JULY 2000

The Dutch football association, the Koninklijke Nederlandse Voetbalbond, are backing Ireland's proposal to jointly host Euro 2008 with Scotland.

MONDAY 22ND JULY 1946

Turlough O'Connor, who was born today in Athlone, played in the LOI, predominantly for Bohemians, before moving to England and Fulham, where he was playing on his Irish debut in 1967. He only manages a lone appearance for Fulham but goes on to win six caps and later becomes a successful manager in Ireland.

TUESDAY 23RD JULY 1963

One of Irish football's most-capped players, Andy Townsend, who is born today in Maidstone, made more than a century of appearances in the Southern League for Welling before breaking into the professional ranks with Southampton. He later plays for Norwich City, Chelsea, Aston Villa, Middlesbrough and West Bromwich Albion. Townsend is playing at Carrow Road when he makes his international debut in February 1989 against France. He plays in all five matches at the following year's World Cup finals and captains the Irish team that again progress from the group stages at the next finals in 1994. A popular TV pundit, he was the pioneer of the ill-fated Tactics Truck and commentated on the 2010 World Cup finals for ITV.

TUESDAY 24TH JULY 1951

Paddy Moore passes away, aged just 41. Briefly with Shamrock Rovers as a young man, he moved to Britain in 1929, played briefly for Cardiff City, Merthyr Town and Tranmere, then goes back to the Hoops. Two years after his first ill-fated trip to Britain, he leaves for Aberdeen, where in only his seventh league match he scores six times. The year before moving to Scotland he made his debut for Ireland and was only 21 when he played against Spain. Moore silenced the 100,000 crowd at the Montjuich Stadium in Barcelona when, with confidence that belied his years, he chipped the home keeper from outside the penalty area. He later returned to the LOI but died of alcohol-related problems in the English city of Birmingham.

SUNDAY 25TH JULY 1948

Only a day before the game is actually to be played, the Irish amateur team at the Olympics find out who they will play in the first round. If Ireland – managed by Johnny Carey – can beat Holland in their preliminary-round tie tomorrow, their next match is at Arsenal's Highbury Stadium against hosts Great Britain on July 31st.

MONDAY 26TH JULY 1948

After an absence of 24 years, Ireland return to the Olympic Games football tournament and again take on the Netherlands, this time at Portsmouth's Fratton Park. Ireland are two goals down in ten minutes. Bobby Smith of Bohemians pulls a goal back, a minute into the second half, but the Dutch win 3-1 to send Ireland out in the preliminary round.

TUESDAY 26TH JULY 1988

Ireland become the first country to hold the Uefa under-16 and under-18 titles simultaneously after Brian Kerr's team upset Germany to win the latter. In an eight-team tournament, Ireland begin by trouncing Croatia 5-2 but then lose to England as Alan Smith's solitary goal settles the game. In their last match Ireland thump Cyprus 3-0, with Robbie Keane scoring twice, to win the group on goal difference. In the final, Alan Quinn scores first for Ireland on 70 minutes but Andreas Gensler equalises and the game goes to penalties. Alex O'Reilly saves twice for Ireland and Liam George scores the winner in a 4-3 shoot-out to clinch the trophy.

FRIDAY 27TH JULY 1973

Armchair football fans will soon see Ireland in green after the government lifts colour restrictions on RTÉ transmissions.

TUESDAY 28TH JULY 1981

Irish international Tony Grealish completes a £100,000 transfer to Brighton & Hove Albion from Luton Town.

MONDAY 29TH JULY 1963

Jim Beglin was playing in the Central League for Liverpool when he was called up to the Irish squad by Eoin Hand in 1984 and makes his debut in a 1-0 win over China. Born today, Beglin moves into the first XI at Anfield, winning the First Division title and FA Cup in 1985/86 and looked set to become an Irish regular for years until a bad leg break in a League Cup quarter-final with Everton in January 1987. He was only 23. He later moves to Leeds and helps the club win the 1989/90 Second Division title but never recaptures his earlier form and his last Irish cap came in 1987.

MONDAY 30TH JULY 1974

Tony Dunne has been given a free transfer by Manchester United and today signs for Bolton Wanderers, who have just won promotion to the old Second Division. Dunne signs in time to be included in Bolton's three-match tour of Holland and Germany.

WEDNESDAY 31ST JULY 1974

Southampton's Irish international defender Tony Byrne joins Hereford United in an £18,000 transfer.

REPUBLIC OF IRELAND
On This Day

AUGUST

SATURDAY 1st AUGUST 1981

A skilful, hard-working winger, Stephen Patrick Hunt is born today in Laois and grows up in Clonea-Power, Waterford. The older brother of another Irish international, Noel, Stephen plays hurling as a boy and football for Carrick United. Moving to England, he makes little impact at Crystal Palace but proves a big success at Brentford, earning a move in 2005 to Reading, where he gained promotion to the Premier League. The first of many Irish caps comes in a 2-1 win over San Marino in February 2007.

FRIDAY 2nd AUGUST 1957

The Stella Maris club has produced a swathe of talented Irish footballers and Augustine Ashley Grimes, who celebrates his birthday today, is one. A left-footed defender or midfielder, Grimes left Bohemians with a 1976 FAI Cup winners' medal, for Manchester United in 1977 where he made 90 appearances in a six-year spell. His international debut came in 1978 and he won 18 caps, scoring one goal – a rocket against Spain in a 1983 European Championship qualifier – and later played there for Osasuna.

FRIDAY 3rd AUGUST 1945

Eamon Dunphy is best known as an author and modern-day scourge of Ireland managers as a pundit on RTÉ, but he also won 23 caps for Ireland. Dunphy, who was born today, signed for Matt Busby's Manchester United as a 16-year-old but left without making an impact on the first XI for York City, staying only a season but winning his first Irish cap in a 1-0 defeat at home to Spain in a World Cup qualifier. He moved to Millwall, making 274 first-team appearances. The first of many off-field contributions came in 1971, when he led a players' campaign against the role of the archaic selection committee and succeeded in giving Mick Meagan input into selection.

FRIDAY 4th AUGUST 1978

Irish international Maurice Daly is leaving Wolverhampton Wanderers for a new life in Sweden, where he will study civil engineering. The former Drumcondra player has been at Molineux for five seasons and only played a handful of games. In Sweden, he signs for Vasteraas SK and plays for seven seasons before retiring in 1984/85.

FRIDAY 5TH AUGUST 1988

Eddie Nolan, who was born today, has played for Ireland at every level. A defender from Waterford, he made little impact at Blackburn Rovers in a three-year spell but joined Preston North End in 2009 and won his first full cap that year.

THURSDAY 6TH AUGUST 1914

The Moulson family produced two Irish internationals: Con, winner of five caps during the 1930s, and his younger brother George, who was born today. A goalkeeper, George was bought out of the Army by Grimsby Town in 1936 but England international George Tweedy was first choice and Moulson did not make his Football League debut until 1947. His first cap came the next year against Portugal but Ireland lost all three games that George Moulson featured in and he never played for the national team after 1949.

FRIDAY 7TH AUGUST 1914

The birthday of Florrie Burke, also a talented hurler, who joined Cork United in 1942 and won five LOI championships with the club, and captained them to the double in 1950/51. He was made man of the match on his international debut against West Germany in 1952, when Ireland won 3-2, but never played again after getting involved in a dispute with his club.

WEDNESDAY 8TH AUGUST 1984

Mexico hold Ireland to a 0-0 draw in a friendly watched by a paltry crowd of just 5,000 at Dalymount Park.

SATURDAY 8TH AUGUST 1987

Paul McGrath and Liam Brady are among the starting XI for a Football League representative side that take on a side featuring Diego Maradona, and billed as the Rest of the World, at Wembley Stadium. A 61,000 crowd see the hosts ease home 3-0 with Maradona barely getting near the ball after an acclaimed performance by McGrath. Bobby Robson had chosen the home side and makes a host of substitutions but McGrath and Brady play the entire game. "In the dressing room afterwards, I felt ten feet tall," recalls McGrath. "The boys were full of it. 'Diego f***** who?'"

TUESDAY 9TH AUGUST 1949

Born today, Don Givens is one of Ireland's best-ever footballers. Coming from a Limerick family, where hurling and Gaelic football were the favoured sports, Givens begins playing football as a schoolboy with Dublin side Rangers. By 17, he had been snapped up by Manchester United but was surprisingly released after only a handful of games by Wilf McGuinness. The mistake would be Old Trafford's loss as Givens goes on to great success with Luton Town, Queens Park Rangers and Birmingham City and lights up Irish football during a poor period. He won 56 caps for Ireland and scored 19 goals and later played in Switzerland for Neuchatel Xamax, where he moved into coaching. He has twice been caretaker manager of the Irish national team in 2002 and 2007/08 and managed the under-21 side for a decade.

MONDAY 10TH AUGUST 1970

After more than 350 appearances for Manchester United, Republic of Ireland full-back Shay Brennan moves to Waterford and takes over as player-manager.

TUESDAY 10TH AUGUST 1971

Roy Keane is born at 88 Ballinderry Park in Mayfield, Cork, to Maurice and Marie Keane. He is the fourth of five children and later moves to Lotamore Park. A Spurs fan as a boy, he is playing under-11 football by the age of nine for Rockmount AFC alongside Paul McCarthy, Alan O'Sullivan, Damien Martin and Len Downey, who would also later play for Ireland at some form of representative level. Rejected by Cork City for being too small, he asks for trials at English clubs including Aston Villa, Chelsea and Derby County, to no avail. He joins Cobh Ramblers but is soon spotted by Brian Clough and signs for Nottingham Forest, staying for three seasons before Manchester United pay £3.75 million for his services. He wins numerous trophies but misses out on a Champions League winner's medal when he gets a yellow card for tripping Zinedine Zidane in the semi-final with Juventus and has to miss United's final win over Bayern Munich. His performance in the semi-final is described by United manager Sir Alex Ferguson as the "most emphatic display of selflessness". One of Ireland's greatest players, he wins 66 caps for Ireland and after retiring goes into management.

THE AVIVA, THE NEW HOME OF IRISH FOOTBALL, WHICH ON WEDNESDAY 11TH AUGUST 2010 HOSTED ITS FIRST FOOTBALL INTERNATIONAL WITH IRELAND TAKING ON ARGENTINA.

MONDAY 11TH AUGUST 1923

A fair few players born outside of Ireland have played for the Irish national team but Sean Byrne, who died today, went in the opposite direction. A goalscoring midfield player for St Patrick's Athletic then Dundalk, where he won the double in 1978/79, Byrne went with the LOI on a tour of New Zealand in the summer of 1982. He soon emigrated to New Zealand, played for Gisborne City and after taking out citizenship won four caps for the All Whites. He later moved to Australia, where he coached Morwell Pegasus but died of motor neurone disease in his fifties.

FRIDAY 11TH AUGUST 1967

The Irish amateur team host the Great Britain Olympic team at Dalymount Park in a friendly international but go down 2-0.

WEDNESDAY 11TH AUGUST 2010

The Aviva Stadium, Irish football's new home, stages its first international as Ireland lose 1-0 to Argentina. A joint venture between the FAI and the Irish Rugby Football Union, the 50,000-seat stadium cost €410 million to build with the Irish government stumping up €191 million.

SUNDAY 12TH AUGUST 1962

After a bye in the first round, Ireland's Nations Cup campaign gets underway with a home tie against Iceland at Lansdowne Road. Goals from Liam Tuohy, Ambrose Fogarty and a brace from Noel Cantwell win a thrilling game 4-2.

WEDNESDAY 12TH AUGUST 2009

Australian Tim Cahill has a Samoan mother and a grandmother from Cork and Ireland wish he was on their side today as the Everton player scores twice in Australia's 3-0 thrashing of Ireland in a rare international in Limerick.

WEDNESDAY 13TH AUGUST 1986

Plenty of Irish internationals have come from Britain but Joseph Lapira was born today in Rochester, New York. His career has taken him from the Louisiana Outlaws to Norwegian side Nybergsund IL-Trysil and in 2007 he won his first Irish cap against Ecuador.

MONDAY 14TH AUGUST 2000

Ireland move up one place in the updated Fifa rankings without playing a game to sit joint 38th with Iran and Zambia!

WEDNESDAY 15TH AUGUST 2001

Two late Croatian goals from Davor Vugrinec and Davor Suker deny Ireland a win after Damien Duff and Clinton Morrison had put Mick McCarthy's team 2-0 up in a friendly at Lansdowne Road.

WEDNESDAY 16TH AUGUST 1922

Born today, Peter Farrell played for Northern Ireland and the Republic, captaining the latter during an 11-year spell that saw the chunky wing-half win 28 caps. Originally with Glasthule boys' club, Farrell was picked up by Shamrock Rovers before he was even 17 and despite his youth he was taken on Ireland's historic post-war tour of Iberia in 1946, making his debut in the first game against Portugal. His career is closely associated with Tommy Eglington. The two play together at Shamrock Rovers then leave for Everton in 1946 with Farrell going on to play 421 times for the Merseyside team. His last Irish cap came in the 5-1 hammering by England and he joined Tranmere that year. Peter Farrell passed away in March 1999, aged 76.

WEDNESDAY 16TH AUGUST 2006

Ireland have had many close games with Holland over the years but today is not one of them as Marco van Basten's side post a 4-0 win at Lansdowne Road in Steve Staunton's third game as manager.

WEDNESDAY 17TH AUGUST 2005

A 44,000 crowd at Lansdowne Road see Ireland kick off their season with a tough friendly against Italy, who take the lead and are soon 2-0 up. Andrew Reid quickly pegs Italy back but the visitors triumph 2-1.

WEDNESDAY 18TH AUGUST 2004

Andrew Reid puts Brian Kerr's team 1-0 up against Bulgaria at Lansdowne Road but a second-half goal from Valeri Bojinov ensures parity and a draw for the visitors.

SATURDAY 19TH AUGUST 2000

Tony Cascarino's career is finally over. He terminates his contract with French side Red Star after being substituted in only his second (and final) game of the season. "The team were an absolute disaster," recalls Cascarino. A week later, Red Star ask him to return but after well over 600 club appearances and 88 internationals for Ireland, Cascarino is done.

WEDNESDAY 20TH AUGUST 1997

Lithuania prove resolute opponents at Lansdowne Road today and restrict Ireland to a 0-0 draw in a World Cup qualifier.

WEDNESDAY 21ST AUGUST 2002

Mick McCarthy's team get their season off to a flying start as goals from Robbie Keane, Colin Healy and Graham Barrett are enough to rout Finland 3-0 in a friendly in Helsinki.

MONDAY 22ND AUGUST 1986

That Stephen Ireland became a Premier League player and Irish international is testament to his talent and determination to overcome Osgood-Schlatter disease. Ireland, who was born today, had trials with many British clubs as a teenager, when he was plagued with the knee complaint. Born on this day, 14 years later he is signed by Manchester City and makes the first XI in 2005. He won the first of six Irish caps the next year but has not played since 2007 after fabricating his grandmother's death as a reason for missing a game.

WEDNESDAY 22ND AUGUST 2007

A brace apiece from Robbie Keane and Shane Long give Steve Staunton's team a reassuring 4-0 win in Copenhagen over Denmark.

WEDNESDAY 23RD AUGUST 1961

Pip Meighan becomes the first Irish referee to take charge of an international in Continental Europe, when he officiates in a World Cup qualifier between Norway and Russia in Oslo. The Russians win 3-0 and Meighan is later put forward for the inaugural Soccer Writers' Association Personality of the Year award but loses out to Drumcondra centre forward, Dan McCaffrey.

WEDNESDAY 23RD AUGUST 1995

John Joseph Carey, known more commonly as Johnny or Jackie, passes away in Macclesfield, England, aged 76. One of the great stars of Irish football of any era, he was born in Dublin on February 23rd 1919. His parents wanted Carey to go to university but he joins St James's Gate at the start of the 1936/37 season. Within two months he has been snapped up by Manchester United for £250. He wins 29 caps for Ireland between 1937 and 1953 and nine for Northern Ireland after the war. Carey was the first non-Englishman to captain a team to both the FA Cup and the First Division title. Manchester United manager Sir Matt Busby rated him on a par with Bobby Charlton and George Best. In 1949, he was voted Football Writers' Association Player of the Year.

FRIDAY 24TH AUGUST 1962

A defender Peter Eccles, who was born today, made his solitary Irish appearance in 1986 in a 1-1 draw with Uruguay. Eccles later leaves Shamrock Rovers for Leicester City, where he is substituted at half-time in his only game. Returning to the Hoops, he is 1993 Player of the Year and leads the team to the 1993/94 double but never returns to the Ireland side.

SATURDAY 25TH AUGUST 1990

After reaching that summer's World Cup quarter-finals, Ireland reach a then record number seven in Fifa's rankings.

FRIDAY 26TH AUGUST 1932

Dermot Patrick Curtis, who was born today, was a prolific goalscorer with Shelbourne, Bristol City and Exeter City, where he helped the Grecians win promotion in 1963/64 and became the club's first international. He featured 17 times for Ireland, scoring eight goals.

THURSDAY 27TH AUGUST 1970

Born today, Jeffrey Jude Kenna played three times for Ireland at under-21 level before he even featured for the first team at Southampton. A full-back, he joins Blackburn Rovers in 1995 for £1.5 million and goes on to win 27 full caps for Ireland.

MONDAY 28TH AUGUST 1939

Six members of the Hale family played for Waterford, including Alfie, a sharp forward who won 14 caps for Ireland. His performance for the Irish Olympic team in a 6-3 win over Holland in 1960 prompts Aston Villa to sign Hale for £4,500. He is hampered by niggling injuries but makes his full international debut in 1962 against Austria before leaving Villa Park for Doncaster Rovers, then Newport County. In 1966, he returns to the LOI and the Blues, winning five titles. After making a brief comeback in the 1980s with Thurles Town, he has the distinction of having scored in four decades; the 1950s, 1960s, 1970s and 1980s.

MONDAY 28TH AUGUST 2000

Phil Babb and Mark Kennedy are in Garda custody at Harcourt Terrace Station on charges of causing criminal damage to a car. The next day, Ireland manager Mick McCarthy drops both players from this week's crucial World Cup qualifier with Holland. After paying an IR£950 fine, the pair face the media at their own volition. "I would like to apologise to the young lady for the damage done to her car," says a chagrined Babb.

SUNDAY 29TH AUGUST 1976

Stephen Carr is born in Dublin. Another product of the celebrated Stella Maris youth set-up, he joins Spurs in 1991. After breaking into the first team two years later, he makes 226 appearances. His international debut came in 1999 and he wins 44 caps but misses the 2002 World Cup due to injury. He joins Newcastle United in 2004 but after struggling with fitness, he is released by manager Kevin Keegan in 2008. Linked with a string of clubs including Aston Villa, Hertha Berlin and Bohemians, he surprisingly retires. Even more surprisingly, he is tempted out of retirement the next year by Birmingham City, becomes captain and leads the club to its best-ever Premier League finish.

WEDNESDAY 30TH AUGUST 2000

A depleted Irish under-18 team are outclassed 3-1 by Germany in the first of two friendlies in Gutersloh. "We played well enough but it was a good German side," admits manager Brian Kerr.

WEDNESDAY 31st AUGUST 1977

Ian Harte, who is born today, made his Football League debut for Leeds United alongside his uncle, Gary Kelly. Harte was only 18 and Kelly just 21! Harte had only played four times for Leeds when he was given a start for Ireland in 1996 by Mick McCarthy and goes on to win 64 caps over the next 11 years. He was ever-present in Ireland's successful qualification for the 2002 World Cup finals. After nine years and 213 games for Leeds United, he left the financially stricken Yorkshire club for Spanish side Levante in 2004 and stays three years before returning to play for Sunderland, then Blackpool and more recently Carlisle United.

SATURDAY 31st AUGUST 1996

A day for coincidences as Ireland visit Vaduz and thrash Liechtenstein 5-0 in a World Cup qualifier through goals from Keith O'Neill, Ian Harte and a brace from Niall Quinn. The other Irish goal is scored by captain Andy Townsend, formerly of Southampton. That same day, England, Northern Ireland and Wales are also in action in World Cup qualifiers and also led by former Saints players. Alan Shearer leads England, Iain Dowie takes charge on the field for Northern Ireland and Barry Horne captains Wales.

THURSDAY 31st AUGUST 2000

Noel King is appointed manager of the Irish senior women's team.

FRIDAY 31st AUGUST 2001

The day before Ireland's penultimate World Cup qualifying group game, Fifa make the draw for the play-offs for teams finishing second. Ireland have every chance of a play-off spot and discover they will play an as yet unknown team from Asia.

REPUBLIC OF IRELAND
On This Day

SEPTEMBER

SATURDAY 1st SEPTEMBER 1923

The Irish Free State Football Association (IFSFA) is granted full membership of Fifa. The IFSFA had been given provisional membership earlier in the year despite pressure on Fifa from the four British Home Nations.

SATURDAY 1st SEPTEMBER 1962

Tony Cascarino is born in Orpington, Kent and goes on to win 88 caps for Ireland. "Why did I choose the Republic of Ireland?" he asks rhetorically in his autobiography, *The Secret Life of Tony Cascarino*. "Well, to be honest because they chose me." His grandparents, Agnes and Michael Joseph O'Malley, were from Westport in County Mayo but emigrated to England with their teenage daughter Theresa, Cascarino's mother. "Because we were closer to the O'Malleys than the Cascarinos, I grew up with a strong sense of Irishness," he adds. He starts his career at Gillingham in 1981 and breaks into the Irish side four years later. He went on to play for Millwall, Aston Villa, Celtic and Chelsea before finishing his career in France with Marseille and Nancy, finally retiring in 2000.

SATURDAY 1st SEPTEMBER 2001

Still unbeaten in their quest for a place at next year's World Cup finals, Mick McCarthy's men know that a win today against Holland will ensure the play-offs at least. For McCarthy, the game is the biggest of his life but injury deprives him of Mark Kinsella, Stephen Carr, Kenny Cunningham, Gary Breen and Ian Harte. The Dutch have lost Edgar Davids to a five-month drugs ban but those Irish players fit enough to play do not let their country down. A tight match is goalless at half-time then on 58 minutes, Gary Kelly chops down Marc Overmars for a second yellow card. Ireland are down to ten men. A draw should still see Ireland to a play-off slot but minutes later Jason McAteer scores what proves to be the winner with a half-volley.

SUNDAY 2nd SEPTEMBER 1962

When Liam Tuohy puts Ireland ahead after 38 minutes in Reykjavik, the Newcastle United outside-left's goal is the first away goal by an Irishman in what will become the European Championship. Iceland equalise in the second half but Ireland go through 5-3 on aggregate.

MONDAY 2ND SEPTEMBER 1974

Irish international Johnny Giles wants to talk to new Leeds United boss Brian Clough about his future – already.

SATURDAY 2ND SEPTEMBER 2000

Mick McCarthy asked for Holland or Portugal in their first World Cup qualifier and got the Dutch, whose coach Frank Rijkaard is stepping down after Euro 2000. Dennis Bergkamp has retired. Louis van Gaal has been successful in charge of Ajax and Barcelona but this is his first competitive game as Holland coach. "No matter how experienced you are in the club game, you just cannot step up to the world stage and take to it immediately," says McCarthy. Ireland take the lead on 21 minutes as Robbie Keane finishes off a flowing move. Jason McAteer adds another but Ireland drop off, allowing two late goals to rescue a point for the hosts.

SATURDAY 3RD SEPTEMBER 1955

Six Irish internationals are on the field at Goodison Park, when Everton play Luton Town in a First Division fixture and the newly promoted Hatters, whose XI includes Seamus Dunne, Tommy Aherne and George Cummins spring a surprise with a 1-0 win. Everton's Irishmen are Tommy Eglington, Frank O'Farrell and Jim O'Neill.

FRIDAY 4TH SEPTEMBER 1998

Ireland's under-21 team draw 2-2 with Croatia in a European Championship qualifier in Kilkenny.

SATURDAY 5TH SEPTEMBER 2009

"The performance over 90 minutes was depressing; it exposed the limitations of the coach's philosophy," signs RTÉ critic Eamon Dunphy after Ireland squeeze out a 2-1 win over Cyprus in a World Cup qualifier. Ireland are 38th in the world, Cyprus 76th, but only an 83rd-minute goal from Robbie Keane – his fortieth at international level – saves Giovanni Trapattoni. "When kids see Lionel Messi, Steven Gerrard or Ronaldo they want to go out in the park and do what they've seen the guys do the night before," fumes Dunphy in comments picked up by thesportsreview. com. "Nobody wants to go out in the park in the morning and hit the ball 60 yards up in air."

TUESDAY 6TH SEPTEMBER 1983

Stephen Michael Kelly is born in Finglas and joins the Spurs youth programme, making more than 40 appearances before signing for Birmingham City. A right-back, he later plays for Stoke City, then Fulham, and wins his first cap for Ireland in 2006.

TUESDAY 7TH SEPTEMBER 1971

Women's football in Ireland is dealt a blow after world body Fifa rules it wants nothing to do with the sport anywhere.

THURSDAY 8TH SEPTEMBER 1949

Regulars are missing for Ireland's game with Finland at Dalymount Park as their English clubs will not release them. New caps Arthur Fitzsimmons, Peter Desmond and Johnny Gavin join the old faces for the pre-match ritual of lunch at Dublin's Gresham Hotel. Gavin marks his debut by opening the scoring and Con Martin marks his 12th cap with a brace for a 3-0 win that is Ireland's first World Cup victory.

WEDNESDAY 8TH SEPTEMBER 1976

David O'Leary makes his debut against England at Wembley. Stuart Pearson gives Don Revie's England the lead but Gerry Daly confidently dispatches a penalty past Ray Clemence to equalise on 52 minutes after Ray Wilkins brings down Steve Heighway. Well marshalled by player-manager Johnny Giles, Ireland draw 1-1.

WEDNESDAY 8TH SEPTEMBER 1993

Ireland play their penultimate qualifier for the 1994 World Cup as Lithuania visit Lansdowne Road. If Ireland win, a solitary point from their last two qualifiers will be sufficient for a trip to the US but David O'Leary is injured and Andy Townsend, Kevin Moran and Niall Quinn are all struggling with hamstring problems. Then Terry Phelan goes down with tonsillitis, while Tommy Coyne is out after his wife died tragically over the summer. With Paul McGrath serving a one-match ban, manager Jack Charlton mulls over moving Roy Keane to centre-half until Moran recovers. Lithuania provide a stern test but first-half goals from John Aldridge and Alan Kernaghan book a 2-0 win and the points. "The irony is that [Lithuania] did to us what we had done to others so often in the past," said Charlton.

SATURDAY 8TH SEPTEMBER 2007

Grannygate: Ireland draw a Euro 2008 qualifier with Slovakia 2-2 in Bratislava. Stephen Ireland scores the opener but will not feature again. Ireland cannot make the next game four days later because his granny has died – except both grandmothers are alive and well. After receiving hate mail, Ireland explains his girlfriend was having a miscarriage but did not want everyone to know so said his grandmother had died. "She just wanted me home and she didn't want to tell a complete stranger that she'd had a miscarriage," he tells the *Daily Telegraph*. "My girlfriend was young. I was young. I didn't want to tell everyone my private business. Not only that, I couldn't turn around and say my girlfriend was lying. I had to stand by her."

WEDNESDAY 9TH SEPTEMBER 1981

The Irish need wins in their last two games to take one of the two qualification slots for next year's World Cup finals. Today's opponents Holland need a result, too, as defeat for either team at the Feyenoord Stadium in Rotterdam is the end for the loser. Frans Thijssen puts the Dutch ahead but Michael Robinson equalises, his strike providing the 100th away goal scored by Ireland. In a thrilling game, Arnold Muhren restores the home lead with a 65th-minute penalty. Six minutes later, Mark Lawrenson beats two players and sends over a cross that Frank Stapleton converts: 2-2, Ireland are still alive – just.

WEDNESDAY 9TH SEPTEMBER 1992

Ireland play their second World Cup qualifier in front of a 32,000 crowd at Lansdowne Road. Latvia are the visitors. "Normally, it is possible to get a line on the strength of a team, even if you've never seen them play," wrote Jack Charlton. "But in this instance that simply wasn't possible." The Latvians had held group rivals Denmark to a draw in Riga, a result that "shocked" Charlton and after 30 minutes, the game is goalless until Kevin Sheedy settles his manager's nerves by hammering home a Denis Irwin cross. Ireland begin to dominate and a second-half hat-trick from John Aldridge seals a comfortable 4-0 win.

WEDNESDAY 10TH SEPTEMBER 1980

Eoin Hand takes charge of Ireland in a competitive match for the first time today, leading his new charges out against Holland in a World Cup qualifier. Hand is just 34 but in his first season as a player-manager he won the title with Limerick and was voted Ireland's soccer Personality of the Year by the country's journalists. Ireland are in a group including Belgium and France but recover from Simon Tahamata's early goal to produce a famous 2-1 triumph over the 1978 World Cup finalists with goals from Gerry Daly and Mark Lawrenson. The match is also notable for Pierce O'Leary's appearance – the last by a LOI player in a World Cup match.

WEDNESDAY 10TH SEPTEMBER 1986

After winning the Iceland tournament, Ireland's new manager turns his attention to qualification for the 1988 European Championships and Jack Charlton's side do not let him down at the Heysel Stadium. Frank Stapleton pegs back Belgium's early lead and a Liam Brady penalty levels the scores for a 2-2 draw and a point against the 1980 runners-up.

TUESDAY 11TH SEPTEMBER 1979

Ireland play their 100th friendly international, taking on Wales in Swansea. Joey Jones puts through his own net on 22 minutes but Ian Walsh equalises minutes later and Alan Curtis wins the match for Wales in the second half.

WEDNESDAY 11TH SEPTEMBER 1985

Tony Cascarino plays his first game for Ireland in a World Cup qualifier at the Wankdorf Stadium in Berne. Cascarino forced his way into Eoin Hand's thinking after an impressive performance for a Glenn Hoddle XI in a testimonial in Dublin during the summer for former Irish international Jimmy Holmes. Cascarino recalls being thrilled to meet Liam Brady, who invited him into the team's card school and promptly won the debutant's match fee. Cascarino buys new boots for the occasion, which give him blisters. The game ends 0-0.

WEDNESDAY 12TH SEPTEMBER 1984

Ireland start their 1986 World Cup qualification campaign with a 1-0 win over Russia at Lansdowne Road, Michael Walsh the scorer.

TUESDAY 12TH SEPTEMBER 1989

John Aldridge agrees to sign for La Liga side Real Sociedad and plans to fly to Spain tomorrow but is surprised to be named as Liverpool substitute in tonight's game with Crystal Palace at Anfield. With Liverpool 5-0 up and awarded a penalty, Peter Beardsley is replaced by Aldridge, who scores from the spot as Liverpool romp home 9-0.

WEDNESDAY 12TH SEPTEMBER 2007

Stephen Hunt – only on the field as a substitute late in the second half – gets himself sent off after 61 minutes for a high tackle as Ireland suffer a frustrating defeat to the Czech Republic in a European Championship qualifier. Marek Jankulovski scores after 15 minutes. Despite Hunt's dismissal, Ireland play well enough to get something from the game. Even home manager Karel Bruckner agrees with Ireland manager Steve Staunton that the red card was severe. "It was very harsh," groans Staunton to *The Guardian*. "Hunt's momentum took him through. There was a lot of play-acting and I was very unhappy with what their centre-half, Radoslav Kovac, said to the referee. Until then it looked like he was only going to give a yellow card. We are bitterly disappointed. We had enough chances to have got something out of the game, even with ten men. These players have only got together for the last 12 months. They have done well so far but they could do better."

MONDAY 13TH SEPTEMBER 1982

Everton defender Mike Walsh is the surprise selection for the Irish squad to take on the Netherlands on September 22nd. Walsh is one of ten English-born players in the 22-man party and only has three caps.

WEDNESDAY 14TH SEPTEMBER 1988

"I see Aldridge has kept a clean sheet again," a journalist remarks in the press box at Windsor Park in Belfast after a 0-0 World Cup qualifying draw between the Republic and their counterparts in the north. The Liverpool striker has not netted for Ireland for 19 games in a row but new manager Jack Charlton will keep the faith.

SUNDAY 15TH SEPTEMBER 2002

FAI hopes of hosting Euro 2008 with Scotland are hit after the collapse of the Irish government's plan to build a 65,000 all-seater stadium on Dublin's western outskirts. After the cost to the Irish taxpayer spiralled to more than €500 million, the stadium plan collapses. "The government has misled the Football Association of Ireland and the Scottish Football Association," Pat Rabbitte, the Labour TD (MP) for Dublin West widely credited with christening the scheme 'Bertie's Bowl' tells *The Guardian*. "It has damaged the image of our country and made a laughing stock out of us. Bertie Ahern thought that Stadium Ireland would be a monument to his memory, it has instead turned out to be a personal disaster for him."

SUNDAY 16TH SEPTEMBER 1962

Ireland's amateur team draw 2-2 with their English counterparts in Dublin in a friendly international.

SUNDAY 17TH SEPTEMBER 2006

A crushing tackle on Shay Given by Marlon Harewood leaves the Ireland goalkeeper with a one centimetre tear in his bowel. The incident occurs while Given is playing for Newcastle United against West Ham United. "The surgeon said he has never seen an injury like this through football," Newcastle manager Glenn Roeder tells the BBC. "Shay would be the first to admit when he sees the pictures that Marlon Harewood thought he had an opportunity to get to the ball. Shay being Shay, as brave as he is, was not going to turn away and not go for the ball. He went for the ball, both of them were trying to get the ball fairly and unfortunately, Shay came off worst."

THURSDAY 18TH SEPTEMBER 1958

John Aldridge is born in Liverpool. A prolific striker at club level, he spends five years with Newport County before joining Oxford United in 1984, where his record of 72 goals in 114 appearances attracts the attention of Liverpool and Ireland. He spends two years at Liverpool before decamping to Real Sociedad in Spain. In a decade-long career with Ireland, Aldridge scores 19 goals in 69 appearances and plays in the 1988 European Championships, and the 1990 and 1994 World Cup finals.

SUNDAY 18TH SEPTEMBER 1938

Ireland will play a record five internationals during 1938/39 and the first today sees Switzerland at Dalymount Park. The Swiss tactics involve taking players out with elbows or bodies. At one point Swiss captain Severino Minelli, his Irish counterpart Jimmy Dunne, and English referee Reg Mortimer are embroiled in a ten-minute row. Dunne eventually concedes that the Swiss can defend how they see fit. On his debut, Paddy Bradshaw scores the fastest-ever Irish international goal then adds another. Further goals from Dunne – the first scored by an Irish captain in an international – and Tom Donnelly see the Swiss charred by a 4-0 roasting.

TUESDAY 18TH SEPTEMBER 1983

Kevin Doyle is born in Adamstown. A forward, he plays for St Patrick's Athletic and Cork City before joining Reading in 2005 and helps the Berkshire Club win promotion to the Premier League. After winning under-21 honours with Ireland, Doyle wins his first of many full caps against Sweden on March 1st 2006 as a substitute. In June 2009, Wolverhampton Wanderers buy Doyle from Reading for £6.5 million.

WEDNESDAY 19TH SEPTEMBER 1973

Nick Colgan, perennial reserve goalkeeper for Ireland, is born today in Drogheda County Louth. Since starting with Drogheda in 1991, Colgan's career took him to 15 or more clubs, many on loan. His longest spell was a five-year run at Hibernian from 1999, when he played more than 100 times and made his eight appearances for Ireland.

WEDNESDAY 20TH SEPTEMBER 1978

Ireland take on Northern Ireland for the first time. The occasion is a European Championship qualifier and both teams need points in what will be a tightly contested group that also includes Denmark and England. The game is poor with visiting keeper Pat Jennings only making two saves. John Hennessy of *The Times* notes that the Dublin police band "played as well as anyone". After the game, both sets of players embrace. "Football at least was a winner in terms of behaviour both on and off the pitch and, so far as one could tell, on the terraces," added Hennessy.

FRIDAY 21st SEPTEMBER 1956

Tony Grealish is born in west London but gets an Irish upbringing through his parents' involvement with the local Gaelic Athletic Association. His footballing career takes in Leyton Orient, Luton Town, Brighton & Hove Albion, West Bromwich Albion, Manchester City, Rotherham United and Walsall. He is only 19 on his debut for Ireland in a friendly with Norway in 1976. A midfielder, he makes 45 Irish appearances, many as captain, and scores eight goals.

WEDNESDAY 21st SEPTEMBER 1949

"Eire, we hope, will give their adversaries a good run for their money, as that is what is needed to weld this England side into a real combination. Big things lie ahead," wrote *The Times* ahead of Ireland's World Cup qualifier at Goodison today. The English fans in a 51,847 crowd expect victory but see their team outplayed by Johnny Carey's marvellous Irish side. After Bert Mozley hacks down Frank Farrell, Con Martin scores the penalty and Farrell made sure of a 2-0 win with a goal five minutes from time. "Every man of Eire was a hero," wrote *The Times* the next day, describing England's performance as a "major disaster".

SUNDAY 21st SEPTEMBER 1969

Today is Ireland's first match with Mick Meagan as manager. Don Givens, then with Luton Town, scores for the home side in a friendly with Scotland, who net through Rangers striker Colin Stein. Watched by a crowd of 27,000 at Dalymount Park, the match finishes 1-1.

WEDNESDAY 21st SEPTEMBER 1983

For once, Ireland's manager Eoin Hand is able to name a squad not bedevilled by injuries for today's European Championship qualifier in Reykjavik but even with victory over Iceland, his side look unlikely to catch Spain or the Netherlands in group seven. "Apart from Ronnie Whelan of Liverpool, it's perhaps the first time in 20 games I'll be able to field my strongest team," says Hand to *The Times*. His players do not let him down: first-half goals from Gary Waddock and Michael Robinson, followed by a goal eight minutes from time by Mike Walsh, complete a 3-0 win.

TUESDAY 22ND SEPTEMBER 1970

Steve Heighway makes his first appearance for Liverpool in a League Cup second-round replay with Mansfield Town and will not have to wait long for his international debut.

WEDNESDAY 22ND SEPTEMBER 1982

Gerry Daly gives Ireland hope of a point as Tony Grealish's side stage a late rally in Rotterdam in a European Championship qualifier against Holland, who had scored after just 40 seconds through Dirk Schoenaker. Ruud Gullit added another in the second half before Daly's strike on 79 minutes from a Liam Brady centre. In a thrilling game, Ireland pile on the pressure in the closing minutes but cannot gain parity.

WEDNESDAY 23RD SEPTEMBER 1970

A day after his first Liverpool start, Steve Heighway makes his international debut in a friendly with Poland in front of a 20,000 crowd at Dalymount Park. Heighway has not been back to Dublin since leaving the country as a 10-year-old with his parents. "Things felt a little strange," he admits. "But I have to say that I have never been made to feel a stranger so far as playing for the international team is concerned. I'm proud to be a member of this team, even though my accent is a long way from being Irish." Heighway finishes on the losing side as the Poles triumph 2-0 with two first-half goals. The 24 hours that Heighway had to wait between his club and international debut is believed to be the shortest ever.

FRIDAY 24TH SEPTEMBER 1954

Marco Tardelli, assistant manager to Giovanni Trapattoni with the Ireland team, is born in Capanne di Careggine, Italy. A midfielder, he won Serie A five times, the European Cup with Juventus, and the 1982 World Cup with Italy, for whom he made more than 80 appearances. He managed Italian youth teams, Inter Milan, Bari and Egypt before joining the FAI in 2008.

WEDNESDAY 24TH SEPTEMBER 1986

Ireland's new striker John Aldridge scores four goals for Oxford United against Gillingham in a League Cup match.

MONDAY 25TH SEPTEMBER 1961

Ronald Whelan is born in Dublin. His father Ronnie senior won two caps for Ireland but Whelan would go on to make 53 appearances for Ireland, playing in the 1988 European Championships and winning the First Division title with Liverpool, where he spent 15 years and made more than 360 appearances. He retired in 1996 after a brief spell with Southend United, whom he also managed.

WEDNESDAY 25TH SEPTEMBER 1963

A place in the quarter-finals of the Nations Cup is within Ireland's grasp after a team missing five first-choice players secure a valiant 0-0 draw with Austria in Vienna in this second-round tie. Three Irish-based players, Bill Browne, Ronnie Whelan and Liam Tuohy, are among five reserves drafted in and the part-timers prove the equal of their full-time peers.

TUESDAY 26TH SEPTEMBER 1961

Arsenal's new signing Frank O'Neill is named in an Ireland squad for the first time. O'Neill, who left Shamrock Rovers for Highbury, is the only uncapped player in the Irish squad for next month's World Cup qualifier with Czechoslovakia.

TUESDAY 27TH SEPTEMBER 1938

Maurice Swan, who was born today in Dublin, won just a single cap for Ireland. A goalkeeper, he played when Ireland take on 1958 World Cup runners-up Sweden in Malmo in 1960. The hosts are two goals up inside half an hour before Seamus Dunne put one past Swan. The game finished 4-1 to Sweden and though Swan, a keeper for Drumcondra, Cardiff City and Hull City, played well, he never featured for Ireland again.

SUNDAY 28TH SEPTEMBER 2008

Three years after Grannygate, Stephen Ireland still has no plans to return to the Irish side. "I've got three young children and my commitments at the moment are to my club and my family," he says in today's *Observer*. "International football takes you away from home, and at the moment I feel I'm better off being away from it. I enjoy my life at the moment and I don't really want to change it though, as I say; 'You should never say never'."

IRELAND DEFEND ANOTHER AUSTRIAN ATTACK IN VIENNA, WHERE A BRAVE DISPLAY BY THE VISITORS ON 25TH SEPTEMBER 1963 SECURED A VALUABLE 0-0 DRAW.

COURTESY OF AGENTUR VOTAVA

TUESDAY 29TH SEPTEMBER 1981

Irish manager Eoin Hand has retained his previous job as manager of Limerick, who put in a spirited showing at Southampton, managing a fine 1-1 draw at The Dell – against a team that were runners-up in the English First Division last season – but go out of the Uefa Cup 4-1 on aggregate.

MONDAY 30TH SEPTEMBER 1946

Taoiseach Eamon de Valera hosts a reception for England, who play in Dublin today. Two days ago, Johnny Carey and Brentford's Billy Gorman had played against the English for Northern Ireland, and do so again in a game that also marked the only occasion Doctor Kevin O'Flanagan played alongside his brother Michael. Both amateurs, the O'Flanagans were dual internationals, representing Ireland at rugby union too. The polyglot Irish side today also includes Manchester City's Billy Walsh, who had been capped by England at schoolboy level. In Belfast two days ago, England thumped Northern Ireland 7-2 but in front of a 32,000 crowd at Dalymount Park the visitors are restricted to a 1-0 win courtesy of a goal on 82 minutes from Tom Finney. The match also saw the return of Alex Stevenson to the Irish team, 14 years after his last game – a 2-0 win against Holland.

REPUBLIC OF IRELAND
On This Day

OCTOBER

THURSDAY 1st OCTOBER 2009

Ireland are likely to miss out on automatic qualification for next year's World Cup finals in South Africa and are heading for a two-legged play-off, which – after a sudden about-turn – Fifa has decided to seed to the dismay of the FAI. "A year ago, we were told by Fifa that the play-offs would most likely not be seeded," FAI chief executive John Delaney complains to *The Guardian*. "But a couple of weeks ago, they wrote to us to say that it would now most likely be seeded. We'd have been delighted to be in the play-offs at the start of the group and we'll take what we get."

WEDNESDAY 2nd OCTOBER 1957

A clash of footballing cultures in Copenhagen where Ireland play their final World Cup qualifier. The Irish are already eliminated and Frank O'Farrell and George Cummins replace Ronnie Nolan and Liam Whelan. But, the rest of the starting XI from the previous stirring 1-1 draw with qualifiers England retains their place. Cummins heads Ireland in front on 53 minutes despite Danish protests of an infringement and Dermot Curtis adds another six minutes later. As the game wears on, the home crowd grew incensed that injured Irish players stay on the pitch and wait for a trainer – as is normal in Ireland – instead of following Danish custom and leaving the pitch. The crowd whistle at what they see as time-wasting but Ireland win 2-0.

WEDNESDAY 3rd OCTOBER 1956

Ireland play Denmark for the first time as the two sides clash in their first qualifying match for the 1958 World Cup finals in Sweden. A change in the rules means that all qualifiers must be finished by the November before the finals, hence the early start. For radio commentators, the game was a nightmare as the visitors had two Nielsens, two Jensens and a pair of Hansens. Ireland had the ball in the Danish net early on but English referee Alfred Bond rules Gerry Mackey's strike out for pushing in the box. Dermot Curtis soon puts Ireland ahead despite appearing offside, and Tom Gavin of Norwich added another through a penalty just before half-time. Aage Jensen pulls a late goal back but Ireland hold on for a 2-1 success.

SUNDAY 4TH OCTOBER 1936

Charlie Hurley, central defender for Millwall, Sunderland, Bolton Wanderers and Ireland, is born in Cork. His family move to Essex before his first birthday. Hurley makes his Ireland debut in 1957 and wins 40 caps over the next 11 years and also briefly manages Ireland in the late 1960s.

SUNDAY 4TH OCTOBER 1953

Ireland go down 5-3 at home to France in front of a 45,000 crowd at Dalymount Park in a game that provides the last World Cup cap for Davy Walsh, the only player to have played in the competition for Northern Ireland and the Republic. Walsh played for the North in a World Cup qualifier against Wales in 1950, a year after first playing for Ireland in the same competition against Sweden. Walsh played another World Cup qualifier against France in 1952 before today's final game, when he scores in the 82nd minute. Frank O'Farrell adds another two minutes from time, which on top of Reg Ryan's 58th-minute goal, gives the scoreline some respectability for Ireland.

MONDAY 4TH OCTOBER 1976

Ray Treacy is recalled to the Irish squad for the side's next game, a friendly with Turkey.

MONDAY 5TH OCTOBER 1957

Charlie Hurley makes his debut for Sunderland and the Irish international finishes on the wrong side of a 7-0 hammering from Blackpool in a First Division fixture.

THURSDAY 6TH OCTOBER 1966

The birthday of Niall Quinn, who was born today in Perrystown, Dublin. A talented player at hurling and Gaelic football he eventually focuses on football, and after playing for Manortown United as a youth he is picked up by Arsenal in 1983 – the same year that he plays in the All-Ireland Minor Hurling Championship with Dublin. In a seven-year stint with Arsenal, he plays less than 70 games and moves to Manchester City in 1990, spending six years there then leaving for Sunderland, where he spent a similar amount of time. Quinn made more than 200 appearances for both clubs and won 92 caps for Ireland, scoring 21 goals.

SATURDAY 6TH OCTOBER 1973

Liam Brady makes his Arsenal debut in a 1-0 First Division win over Birmingham City. He is just 17. He wins the FA Cup with the north London club six years later and, after retiring, comes back to the club in 1996 as head of youth development.

WEDNESDAY 6TH OCTOBER 1993

A week to go before Ireland's make-or-break penultimate World Cup qualifier in Spain and the injuries are starting to pile up. Andy Townsend is already out and John Aldridge is reportedly struggling with a hamstring but a call today from the Tranmere player to Jack Charlton puts his international manager at ease. Aldridge subsequently has another problem in training and club boss Johnny King pulls him out of the next day's league game to save the striker for Ireland's big day.

SATURDAY 6TH OCTOBER 2001

Ireland thrash Cyprus 4-0 at Lansdowne Road through goals from Ian Harte, Niall Quinn, David Connolly and Roy Keane, whose majestic display is the game's focal point. After the game, Keane feels that the squad are being treated as second-class citizens by the FAI and lets them know – in no uncertain terms. "Where we trained last Monday, in Clonshaugh, was abysmal and it has been for as long as I've known it," fumes Keane. "I was fairly critical about our seating arrangements on the flight out here, when the officials were sitting in the first-class seats and the players were sitting behind. For me, that's simply not right and it's not just because I'm playing for Manchester United. The priority has to be the team – and I don't think that has always been the case here."

TUESDAY 7TH OCTOBER 1969

Former international Mick Meagan has become Ireland's first full-time manager and today is his first competitive match. The Irish have lost their first three World Cup qualifiers and Meagan starts an 'I'm backing Ireland' campaign. Alfie Hale of Waterford and Joe Kinnear of Tottenham Hotspur are handed debuts but Meagan cannot halt the slide, with Czechoslovakia winning 3-0 through a first-half hat-trick from Jozef Adamec.

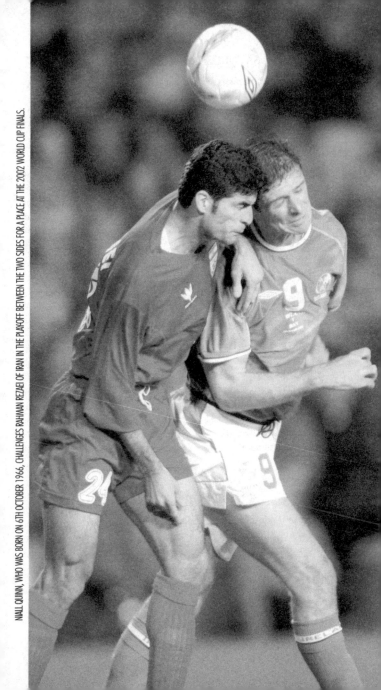

NIALL QUINN, WHO WAS BORN ON 6TH OCTOBER 1966, CHALLENGES RAHMAN REZAEI OF IRAN IN THE PLAYOFF BETWEEN THE TWO SIDES FOR A PLACE AT THE 2002 WORLD CUP FINALS.

SATURDAY 7TH OCTOBER 2000

The last time Ireland played in the Stadium of Light in Lisbon, Mick McCarthy stood on the rain-soaked terraces as Jack Charlton's makeshift side were thrashed 3-0. Now McCarthy is in the dug-out. A positive result today against Portugal would put Mick McCarthy's team in a strong World Cup qualifying position but Portugal will not be surprised so easily, having seen the fine Irish draw in the last match. Alan Kelly saves well from Sa Pinto and Luis Figo before Conceicao puts Portugal ahead on 58 minutes only for Matt Holland to rifle home from 25 yards for another vital point.

SATURDAY 7TH OCTOBER 2006

An infamous day for Irish football, and Steve Staunton's fledgling career as an international manager, sees Ireland comprehensively thrashed in a European Championship qualifier by Cyprus. Shay Given, Steven Reid, Graham Kavanagh, Stephen Carr and Kevin Doyle are missing but the large contingent of travelling Irish fans in the 12,000 crowd at the GSP Stadium still expect better than this embarrassing performance that sees Ireland lose 5-2. Richard Dunne was sent off 12 minutes from time.

SUNDAY 8TH OCTOBER 1961

If Ireland can get at least a point off Czechoslovakia today, then Scotland – the other team in their World Cup qualification group – will go to the finals in Chile. Ireland are out of the running but need to restore some pride after two heavy defeats against the Scots. The Shamrock Rovers pair, Ronnie Nolan and Frank O'Neill, come into the starting XI today but the Czechs score after just three minutes at Dalymount Park. Johnny Giles levels the scores on 40 minutes but Ireland have no answer to the visitors' 4-2-4 formation in the second half and are sunk 3-1 – to the dismay of everyone in Scotland.

SUNDAY 9TH OCTOBER 1949

Ireland play a side that has never gained a World Cup qualifying point, or even scored a goal. In front of a sparse 13,437 crowd at Helsinki's giant Olympic Stadium, Everton's Peter Farrell raised Irish hopes of both points but a minute from time, Vaihela scores his first World Cup goal as the Finns claim their first point.

WEDNESDAY 9TH OCTOBER 1957

The Football League traditionally names virtually a full England side for their annual fixture with the LOI but that all changes today. Instead, a number of untried younger players are given a chance in tonight's game at Elland Road in Leeds. Only one of the starting home XI owns a full cap. An Irish team drawn predominantly from Drumcondra and Shamrock Rovers – and with Alan Kelly in goal – play the better football but are still downed 3-1.

SATURDAY 9TH OCTOBER 1999

Ireland are just 12 seconds away from qualifying for next summer's European Championship finals in Belgium and the Netherlands. Mick McCarthy's side are 1-0 up against Macedonia in Skopje. The game is virtually over but Macedonia – with nothing to play for bar pride – win a final corner. "All we have to do is survive one last corner and I can finally say I have made it as an international manager," recalls McCarthy. The ball swings over, hits Goran Stavervsks and whizzes past Alan Kelly in the Irish goal. The referee blows his whistle moments later. The game finishes 1-1. Direct qualification is gone and Ireland must negotiate a play-off with Turkey.

MONDAY 9TH OCTOBER 2009

At a draw in Fifa's headquarters in Zurich for the final play-off that stands between Ireland and a place at the 2010 World Cup finals, the Irish are unseeded and paired with 1998 winners France.

SUNDAY 10TH OCTOBER 1937

Ireland's second attempt to qualify for the World Cup finals begins on this day. The Irish opponents are Norway, who had produced the shock of the previous year's Olympic football tournament by eliminating hosts and favourites Germany. The teams play each other over two legs. The 32-year-old Jimmy Dunne has returned from England, where he had played for Sheffield United, Arsenal, and Southampton, and signed for Shamrock Rovers. After Matty Geoghegan cancels out Norway's opener, Dunne gives Ireland the lead in the second half but the Norwegians recover to bag a 3-2 win in the first leg at the Ullevaal Stadium.

WEDNESDAY 10TH OCTOBER 2000

After two draws in their difficult opening World Cup 2002 qualifying fixtures, Ireland play their first home game today against Estonia at Lansdowne Road. Only Derby County goalkeeper Mart Poom is recognisable to home fans and after being underdogs in their first two games, Ireland are now firm favourites to win. Ireland have played 18 European and World Cup qualifiers in Dublin and have yet to lose a match. With the same Irish XI that started against Portugal taking the field, a defeat to Estonia would be a huge upset but Alan Kelly is soon called into action before Mark Kinsella puts Ireland ahead on 25 minutes with a close-range shot. Richard Dunne bundles the ball into the net on 51 minutes to complete a 2-0 victory.

SATURDAY 10TH OCTOBER 2009

A last-minute goal from Fiorentina's Alberto Gilardino denies Ireland victory in a World Cup qualifier. Glenn Whelan had opened the scoring on eight minutes but Italy reply and the game is heading towards a draw until Sean St Ledger scores three minutes from time to briefly raise Irish hopes.

WEDNESDAY 11TH OCTOBER 1961

Three days after turning out for Ireland in a World Cup qualifier, the Shamrock Rovers duo, Ronnie Nolan and Frank O'Neill, feature in a League of Ireland representative XI that take on the Football League at Bristol Rovers' Eastville stadium. The pair were the only home-based players in the last Ireland game and Nolan puts through his own net today as the FAI side go down 5-2.

WEDNESDAY 11TH OCTOBER 1989

Ireland are three points clear in second place in World Cup qualifying group six and a place in the finals surely beckons. Northern Ireland – today's visitors to Lansdowne Road – are out of the running after losing to Hungary in their last game but the Hungarians need to beat Spain twice to qualify. Northern Ireland put George Dunlop in goal after a three-year absence and the Linfield keeper picks the ball out of the net three times as Ronnie Whelan, Tony Cascarino and Roy Houghton rack up a 3-0 victory.

MONDAY 12TH OCTOBER 1970

Mick Kearns of Oxford United and Fulham's Jim Conway pull out of the Ireland team for the forthcoming Nations Cup game with Sweden.

SUNDAY 13TH OCTOBER 1963

A Noel Cantwell penalty two minutes from time sends Ireland into the quarter-finals of the European Championship. The Irish drew the first leg of their two-legged tie with Austria 0-0 and lead 2-1 through goals from Cantwell and Ambrose Fogarty until Rudolf Flogel equalises for Austria on 82 minutes. Cantwell is on hand to settle the tie.

WEDNESDAY 13TH OCTOBER 1972

Ireland struggle past Iceland 2-0 in a European Championship qualifier at Lansdowne Road with goals from Frank Stapleton and Tony Grealish.

WEDNESDAY 13TH OCTOBER 1993

John Aldridge has put a poultice on his leg injury but instead of improving his chance of playing in today's vital World Cup qualifier with Spain, the Tranmere player has scalded himself and ruled out any chance of playing. Charlton puts a number ten shirt on Aldridge to keep up the pretence for the visitors, who suspect something is up with the Irish talisman. Unbeaten in the qualifiers, Charlton's team start confidently but within the first half hour the game is over. A Salinas header finds Jose Caminero, who opens the scoring on 11 minutes with a fine volley. Four minutes later Julio Fernandez adds another. "This can't be the game that Javier Clemente and I planned for," says Jack Charlton. "In his case, Christmas has come early. In mine, it's a bloody nightmare." Fernandez adds another on 26 minutes and John Sheridan's second-half goal is merely a consolation. Ireland must go to Belfast for their last qualifier and get a point to qualify for the US.

WEDNESDAY 14TH OCTOBER 1970

Joe Kinnear becomes the first player to come on as a substitute for Ireland in a European Championship match when he replaces Tommy Carroll during today's fixture with Sweden at Dalymount Park. The game finishes 1-1, doing little for Irish hopes of qualification.

WEDNESDAY 14TH OCTOBER 1981

Ireland have drawn and beaten the Netherlands, runners-up in the last two World Cup finals, so far in their qualifying campaign and today must beat France in Dublin. Even that might not be enough as other results have to go Ireland's way to secure the second qualification spot behind Belgium. Eoin Hand's team was one of the strongest in Irish history featuring David O'Leary, Kevin Moran, Mark Lawrenson, Liam Brady, Ronnie Whelan and Frank Stapleton – and victory is achieved. Three minutes from time Don Givens, now with Neuchatel Xamax, comes on for his final Irish cap. In the other qualifier, Holland crush neighbours Belgium 3-0. If the Dutch can draw their final game in Paris against France, Givens' career could end on a high but France win 2-0 then beat Cyprus to confirm Ireland's elimination.

WEDNESDAY 14TH OCTOBER 1992

Ireland travel to the Parken Stadium in Copenhagen with victories in both their opening two qualifiers under their belts, but the new European champions Denmark will be a far tougher prospect than Albania or Latvia. Rain pours out of the sky but there are 8,000 Irish fans in the 40,000 crowd, providing an atmosphere that manager Jack Charlton recalled as "electrifying". Denmark had the Laudrup brothers and Peter Schmeichel, while Ireland had the Northern Ireland-born Alan Kernaghan in only his second international. "Ranged against this kind of talent, we would have to play out of our skins to get a result," added Charlton. They did. A 0-0 draw maintained Ireland's unbeaten start.

WEDNESDAY 15TH OCTOBER 1969

Mick Meagan's Ireland win their first World Cup qualifying point in his fifth game in charge. Don Givens nets after eight minutes. Ireland dominate but visitors Denmark salvage a point after Alan Kelly brings down Begdt Madsen five minutes from the end and Bent Jensen nets from the spot.

WEDNESDAY 15TH OCTOBER 1980

Seven of the Belgian side that reached the final of this year's European Championships turn out for Belgium today in a World Cup qualifier. Belgium score first and although Tony Grealish levels before half-time, Belgium close the game out in the second half for a point.

WEDNESDAY 16TH OCTOBER 1985

"We have left nothing to chance," promises an FAI official ahead of Ireland's journey to Moscow today for a World Cup qualifier with the Soviet Union. "The players do not have to swallow a crumb of Russian food if they so wish. We are travelling with a full kitchen of Irish food – rashers, eggs, black pudding, steaks, ketchup. There can be no excuses on this score." The game is Ireland's 100th competitive match, played in front of a 100,000 crowd, and is goalless at half-time. Eoin Hand's team lose to two second-half goals from Fedor Cherenkov and a last-minute effort from Oleg Protasov.

SATURDAY 17TH OCTOBER 1936

Germany had started the year expecting to win the Olympic football title but, much to Adolf Hitler's displeasure, had been upset in Berlin by Norway and Ireland heap on the embarrassment for Germany today. The game is 2-2 at half-time, Joey Donnelly and Tom Davis of Oldham Athletic on target, but Ireland go on to inflict Germany's heaviest defeat in five years in the second half. Donnelly and Davis are on target again, along with Matty Geoghegan of St James's Gate, for a 5-2 win. Germany do not lose again for two years.

WEDNESDAY 17TH OCTOBER 1979

The brothers David and Pierce O'Leary play together for the first time at senior international level on this day as Ireland trounce Bulgaria 3-0 in a European Championship qualifier at Lansdowne Road. The O'Leary brothers played together three times and on another occasion Pierce came on as a substitute for David during a match against England at Wembley.

WEDNESDAY 17TH OCTOBER 1984

Norway had managed one point from their first three World Cup qualifiers and Eoin Hand's Ireland are confident of getting a result in Oslo today. The Scandinavians had only beaten Ireland once in 11 games – that was a World Cup qualifier – and play with an eight-man defence in front of Erik Thorstvedt. Ireland are poor and when Pal Jacobsen scored on 42 minutes, the defence got even tighter as Norway won out 1-0.

WEDNESDAY 17TH OCTOBER 1990

John Aldridge scores his first international hat-trick as Ireland start their 1992 European Championship qualifying campaign off in style with a whipping of Turkey in front of 46,000 at Lansdowne road. Aldridge opens the scoring. David O'Leary nets before Aldridge hits the target twice more, either side of a Niall Quinn goal for a 5-0 win.

WEDNESDAY 17TH OCTOBER 2007

Today represents a chance for Ireland to gain recompense for one of the national team's most woeful performances, last year's 5-2 thrashing by Cyprus. Steve Staunton desperately needs a win but Cyprus lead 1-0 going into injury time after Stelios Okkarides' goal on 80 minutes. Steve Finnan rescues a point, hardly Staunton's idea of revenge. "I have been given the job and I am going to see it through," Staunton told *The Guardian* on being asked if he had considered his position. "I felt sorry for the fans, and they are within their rights to boo."

THURSDAY 18TH OCTOBER 1923

At a meeting in Liverpool, the four Home Nations and the IFSFA try to reach a compromise over football in Ireland. The International Board – comprised of England, Scotland, Wales and what will later become Northern Ireland – do not want the IFSFA to play internationals and the conference does not produce a solution. England, Scotland and Wales decide the argument should be resolved between the two Irish associations.

TUESDAY 18TH OCTOBER 1955

The Archbishop of Dublin, John Charles McQuaid, protests to the Taoiseach Eamon de Valera over the visit of the national team of communist Yugoslavia for tomorrow's friendly with Ireland, who go down 4-1.

WEDNESDAY 18TH OCTOBER 1972

Alan Kelly becomes the first goalkeeper to captain Ireland, who take on the Soviet Union in the first World Cup qualifier played at Lansdowne Road. Vladimir Fedotov and Viktor Kolotov both score past Kelly in the second half as Ireland go down 2-1 despite Gerry Conroy's late consolation.

FRIDAY 18TH OCTOBER 1974

John Dempsey is one of six Chelsea players booked during a league game at Everton and the Irish international gets himself sent off, after the game finishes, for making remarks to the official. Three days later Dempsey is charged with bringing the game into disrepute, as is his Chelsea teammate Terry Mancini, who starts taking his shorts off as he leaves the pitch.

TUESDAY 18TH OCTOBER 2005

Brian Kerr is axed as Ireland manager, after two-and-a-half years in the post, after last week's scoreless draw in Dublin with Switzerland left his team with no chance of qualifying for the 2006 World Cup.

WEDNESDAY 19TH OCTOBER 1988

After 20 appearances for Ireland, Liverpool striker John Aldridge gets off the mark with a goal in a rout of Tunisia at Lansdowne Road. A brace from Tony Cascarino, and a Kevin Sheedy strike, complete a 4-0 win. "Playing for Liverpool and Ireland could hardly be more different," Aldridge later explains. "At Liverpool I do most of my work in the penalty area. For Ireland, when you're not chasing and closing down defenders, you're chasing the long ball over the top."

SUNDAY 20TH OCTOBER 1957

Ireland's B team play their first official match, beating the Romanian second string 1-0 at Dalymount Park.

MONDAY 20TH OCTOBER 1980

Eoin Hand includes Celtic keeper Packie Bonner and Brighton & Hove Albion's Michael Robinson in the Irish squad for the first time.

WEDNESDAY 21ST OCTOBER 1959

Kevin Sheedy is born – in Builth Wells in Wales. Of Irish descent, Sheedy starts at Hereford United. In four years at Liverpool, he makes a handful of appearances and moves to Everton, where he plays a major role in the club's 1980s successes. "He's so good, he plays as though he were a Brazilian," his former Everton manager Howard Kendall remarked in 1988. Sheedy wins 46 caps for Ireland and plays in the 1990 World Cup finals.

SUNDAY 21st OCTOBER 1973

Johnny Giles' first game as manager of Ireland and his new charges beat Poland 1-0 in a friendly watched by a 25,000 crowd at Dalymount Park. The Polish side is missing Tomaszewski, Gorgon, and Lato, who had recently combined so brilliantly to eliminate England from the World Cup qualifiers at Wembley.

THURSDAY 22nd OCTOBER 1959

The FAI name a team to play Sweden at Dalymount Park on November 1 that is entirely comprised of English-based players.

SUNDAY 23rd OCTOBER 1966

Ireland and Spain fight out a 0-0 draw in the first of four qualifiers for the European Championship in front of a 37,000 crowd at Dalymount Park.

WEDNESDAY 24th OCTOBER 2007

Steve Staunton leaves his job as Ireland manager by mutual consent after an emergency meeting with the FAI. Ireland failed to qualify for Euro 2008 and were thrashed by Cyprus, prompting widespread disillusionment with Staunton. "They have brought through many young players and leave behind a squad with strong development potential," said FAI president David Blood about the departing Staunton and his mentor, Sir Bobby Robson. "As a member of the three-man committee that made the recommendation to appoint Stephen and his team, I am disappointed that things have not worked out the way I, Stephen or my colleagues on the board expected."

SUNDAY 25th OCTOBER 1964

Ireland have not beaten Poland for 26 years. Johnny Carey was in the side that prevailed in 1938 and manages Ireland today in a vintage match for the hosts. Two goals down after just 21 minutes at Dalymount Park, an Irish team featuring four home-based players seem to be missing the injured Johnny Giles but find inspiration in Noel Cantwell, who is not even in the Manchester United first team but drives his teammates on. Blackburn Rovers' Andy McEvoy pulls a goal back four minutes later then sets up a barnstorming finish by equalising eight minutes from time, Jim Mooney scoring the winner on 84 minutes. Mooney's goal is Ireland's 100th home goal.

WEDNESDAY 25TH OCTOBER 1978

A Gerry Daly goal on 27 minutes cancels out Bob Latchford's early strike as Ireland and England fight out a 1-1 draw at Lansdowne Road in a European Championship qualifier.

FRIDAY 26TH OCTOBER 2007

"Jack Charlton ate the job with a giant appetite. Staunton has enjoyed scarcely a peck, but then he does have €750,000 to ease his pain," writes James Lawton in the *Irish Independent* as the pressure on Ireland manager Steve Staunton to stand down grows by the day.

WEDNESDAY 27TH OCTOBER 1965

A draw in Seville today would take Ireland to their first-ever World Cup finals. Andy McEvoy of Blackburn volleys home a Johnny Giles cross on 26 minutes but European champions Spain triumph 4-1. With goal difference not counting, a play-off is needed.

WEDNESDAY 28TH OCTOBER 1953

Ireland's World Cup qualifying hopes revive as Luxembourg are routed at Dalymount Park in a game that sees Tommy Eglington take the captain's armband for the first time. The Grand Duchy had lost all seven of their previous World Cup qualifiers and conceded 36 goals. Arthur Fitzsimmons dribbles round three Luxembourgers for the first on 18 minutes. The visitors stem the Irish tide until Reg Ryan wins and converts a penalty shortly after the break. Fitzsimmons and Eglington finish off a 4-0 win.

WEDNESDAY 28TH OCTOBER 1970

Ireland's European Championship hopes are already looking dim before a Tom Turesson goal a quarter of an hour from time in Stockholm gives Sweden a 1-0 win in today's qualifier.

TUESDAY 28TH OCTOBER 1980

Brighton's Michael Robinson – once Ray Treacy's boot-boy – makes his international debut today as Ireland fall to a 2-0 defeat to France in a World Cup qualifier at Parc des Princes. Robinson's grandmother was born in Ireland but this was not sufficient grounds for qualification in 1980. The rule is parents only so Robinson's mother took out Irish citizenship.

SUNDAY 29TH OCTOBER 1961

A woeful World Cup qualifying campaign ends today with a fourth consecutive defeat and the heaviest yet. At the Strahove Stadium in Prague, Czechoslovakia need two points to force a play-off with Scotland and produce marvellous football to inflict Ireland's biggest-ever World Cup defeat. Four goals down at half-time, Ambrose Fogarty of Sunderland pulls a goal back after the break but the hosts trot out 7-1 winners and go on to make next year's final.

WEDNESDAY 29TH OCTOBER 1975

Simmering tension between the Irish media and Johnny Giles' Irish team escalates after a 4-0 canter over Turkey in a World Cup qualifier at Dalymount Park, where Don Givens scores all four goals – including the fastest-ever hat-trick. After the game, a journalist is bundled out of the victorious Irish team's dressing room by an unidentified but London-based player. "The journalist was also roundly abused in most unparliamentary language," writes Tony Reid in *World Soccer*. "The journalist's 'crime' is not very clear but had the irate international taken the trouble to check his facts more thoroughly he would have discovered that the unfortunate writer whom he abused was not responsible for a story that was, for him, unfortunately alongside his by-line." The offending story claimed that Giles would not drop any of his more established players. This match also marks the last occasion when Ireland fielded a starting XI all born in Dublin.

MONDAY 29TH OCTOBER 1979

Chris Hughton of Tottenham Hotspur is the first black footballer to turn out for Ireland, when he plays in a 3-2 victory over the USA at Dalymount Park. Ireland's goals come in a four-minute blitz started by Tony Grealish in the 64th minute. When Don Givens scores again two minutes later his strike is Ireland's 250th home goal. John Anderson scores the third on 68 minutes.

WEDNESDAY 29TH OCTOBER 1997

Denis Irwin nets after just eight minutes of the home leg of Ireland's World Cup play-off with Belgium but Luc Nilis scores a vital away goal on 30 minutes, and the visitors take a 1-1 draw away from Lansdowne Road.

WEDNESDAY 30TH OCTOBER 1974

Don Givens scores his first international hat-trick as Ireland thrash the Soviet Union 3-0 in a European Championship qualifier at Dalymount Park.

THURSDAY 30TH OCTOBER 2008

The Irish women's side are on the verge of qualifying for the 2009 Uefa finals if they can get a result in Iceland after a 1-1 draw between the two sides four days earlier in Dublin. Ireland finished third behind Sweden and Italy in their qualifying group, which means a play-off with the Icelanders to decide who goes to Finland next year. After being routed 3-0, it will not be Ireland this time.

SUNDAY 31ST OCTOBER 1965

Denis Irwin is born in Cork. He was a fine Gaelic football and hurling player and played at Croke Park as a youth, but preferred football and signed for Leeds United in 1983. He played more than 70 games for Leeds and more than 160 at his next club, Oldham Athletic, where he moved to in 1986 – the year he broke into the Ireland team. Irwin is best remembered for his long, successful career at Manchester United, making more than 360 appearances and winning many honours. In a nine-year international career, he won 56 caps for Ireland. He left Manchester United after a dozen years in 2002 and spent two seasons at Wolverhampton Wanderers before retiring to work in the media for RTÉ and MUTV.

REPUBLIC OF IRELAND
On This Day

NOVEMBER

SUNDAY 1st NOVEMBER 1959

Ireland trail Sweden 2-0 after 16 minutes when a teenage Johnny Giles marks his international debut with a rocket past Bengt Nyholm in the visitors' goal, which prompts an Irish recovery. A Dermot Curtis brace secures a 3-2 win over the previous year's World Cup finalists.

THURSDAY 1st NOVEMBER 1984

Kevin Foley is born in Luton, the son of parents from County Kerry. In May 2004, he makes his debut for Ireland's under-21 team and is FAI under-21 Player of the Year in 2005. In 2007, Foley, a right-back or right-midfielder, leaves his hometown club for Wolverhampton Wanderers – whose manager is former Ireland boss Mick McCarthy – and wins his first Irish cap in a 1-1 draw with Nigeria in 2009.

MONDAY 2nd NOVEMBER 2009

Damien Duff will be available for Ireland's World Cup play-off with France, promises his club manager Roy Hodgson. "It is very hard stopping Damien playing for the Republic of Ireland. You have to lock him in a cage," the Fulham boss tells the BBC.

TUESDAY 3rd NOVEMBER 2009

Irish football fans could miss the second leg of their World Cup play-off with France due to a row over TV rights between RTÉ, Sky Sports, the French Football Federation and their TV partners TF1 over the coverage of the game in Paris on November 18th. Media reports claim that the FFF want €1.5 million for the match after the FAI sold rights to the Dublin game to the highest bidder with independent channel M6 winning with a knockout bid of €4.5 million.

TUESDAY 4th NOVEMBER 1997

Paul McGrath plays his last professional game, turning out for Sheffield United in a 2-2 draw with Ipswich Town at Portman Road. After the match, McGrath told Blades player-manager Nigel Spackman that he was quitting. "Paul, you've got to do what is best for you," McGrath recalls Spackman telling him in his candid autobiography, *Back From The Brink*. "I could detect a small strain of relief in his voice," added McGrath.

WEDNESDAY 5TH NOVEMBER 1969

John Dempsey is the first Irish player to see red after being sent off during a World Cup qualifier with Hungary in Budapest. Hungary need a win to force a play-off with Czechoslovakia. After Lajos Kocsis notches the hosts' third goal, the game boils over. After being penalised for fouling Ferenc Bene, scorer of the second Hungarian goal, Dempsey throws the ball at Yugoslav referee Vlado Jakse. Dempsey is sent off. Lajos Szucs joins him after flattening Ray Treacy.

WEDNESDAY 6TH NOVEMBER 1940

Michael John Giles, player and manager for Ireland and better known as Johnny, is born in Cabra, Dublin. He plays for famous Irish nursery club Stella Maris – Latin for Star of the Sea – then Home Farm before being noticed in 1957 by Billy Behan, the Dublin scout for Manchester United. After the tragic Munich air crash, Giles is one of the players that United rebuild their team around and six days short of his 19th birthday he makes his debut for Ireland. He leaves Old Trafford in 1963 for Leeds United and goes on to win 59 caps for Ireland over the next two decades, taking over as player-manager in 1973.

SUNDAY 6TH NOVEMBER 1960

When Fionan 'Paddy' Fagan scores in a 3-1 friendly victory for Ireland over Norway at Dalymount Park today, he becomes the only player to score in four consecutive games for Ireland. Fagan scored against West Germany, Sweden and Wales (twice). Fagan only won eight Irish caps. Those five goals give him a strike rate of 62.5 per cent.

SUNDAY 7TH NOVEMBER 1937

Norway visit Dalymount Park defending a 3-2 lead from the first leg in Oslo of their World Cup play-off with Ireland but have not come to defend. Jimmy Dunne opens the scoring but by half-time the visitors are 2-1 up and extend that lead shortly after the break. Kevin O'Flanagan scores on his debut to peg the visitors back and Harry Duggan notches his first international goal a minute from time, hammering home a cross from Johnny Carey on his debut – but Norway go through 6-5 on aggregate.

SUNDAY 7TH NOVEMBER 1954

After a Fifa decree, the FAI send out a team known as the Republic of Ireland for the first time. The team fielded by the Belfast-based IFA is now Northern Ireland. In today's game the team formerly known as the Irish Free State and Eire mark their debut (of sorts) beating Norway 2-1 in a friendly at Dalymount Park. Con Martin and Reg Ryan score.

TUESDAY 8TH NOVEMBER 1949

Tommy Moroney pulls out of Ireland's next international on November 13th after the left-half back injures himself in a league match with Tottenham Hotspur at the weekend. His place in the Ireland team to face Sweden goes to Reg Ryan of West Bromwich Albion.

THURSDAY 9TH NOVEMBER 2000

Frustrated at the lack of atmosphere at a recent Champions League game at Manchester United's Old Trafford, Roy Keane makes his feelings known. "Sometimes you wonder," he tells BBC Radio. "Do they understand the game of football? We're 1-0 up, then there are one or two stray passes and they're getting on players' backs. It's just not on. At the end of the day they need to get behind the team. Away from home our fans are fantastic, I'd call them the hardcore fans. But, at home they have a few drinks – and probably the prawn sandwiches – and they don't realise what's going on out on the pitch."

WEDNESDAY 10TH NOVEMBER 1965

Eamon Dunphy makes his Ireland debut at the Colombes Stadium in Paris, which has been such a lucky venue for Ireland in the past. Ireland reached the quarter-finals of the Olympics at Colombes in 1924 and take on Spain there today in a play-off for a place in next year's World Cup finals. The FAI had asked for the play-off to be staged at Wembley. Spain disagree and take 30,000 fans to Paris, where Ireland charge into the attack. Spain soon seize control, restricting Ireland to breakaways and on 79 minutes Jose Ufarte scores the winner. The fixture would be the last World Cup game for Noel Cantwell. He is Ireland's top scorer with 14 goals but has never scored in a World Cup game.

TUESDAY 10TH NOVEMBER 1987

David Kelly becomes the only player to score a hat-trick on his international debut as he rifles home three goals in a 5-0 win over Israel in a friendly game at Dalymount Park.

SATURDAY 10TH NOVEMBER 2001

After beating Bahrain, Iran stand between Ireland and next year's World Cup finals. Mick McCarthy tells the press corps that due to concerns over the security situation in Iran his wife Fiona will be going to Tehran and he will stay at home. For once, injuries are not an issue. Iran have five players across the back and have swamped the midfield. The onus is on Ireland who struggle to break through the Iranian rearguard. Not until the 43rd minute, when Rezaei hacks down Jason McAteer, do Ireland score as Ian Harte thumps home the resulting penalty. Minutes into the second half, a left-foot volley from Robbie Keane doubles the score. Iran finally have to come out of their shell and the talented Ali Daei soon creates a chance for Karimi. More follow but Ireland retain their two-goal advantage for the trip to Tehran.

WEDNESDAY 11TH NOVEMBER 1975

Reaching the 1978 World Cup finals looks tough as a difficult qualifying draw pits the Irish against Bulgaria and France in a three-team group.

WEDNESDAY 11TH NOVEMBER 1987

Joy in Ireland as Jack Charlton's team qualify for their first international tournament courtesy of a late strike from Gary Mackay for Scotland in Sofia knocks Bulgaria out of the running.

THURSDAY 12TH NOVEMBER 1981

The FAI invoke Uefa's rule on international eligibility to make Glasgow Celtic release Packie Bonner for next week's World Cup qualifier with Cyprus. Celtic told the FAI that Bonner was needed for a Scottish Cup semi-final with Dundee United. "We had no option but to invoke the Uefa ruling," FAI secretary Pat O'Driscoll tells *The Times*. The FAI also used the rule against Arsenal, Birmingham City and Tottenham Hotspur to release players for the previous month's qualifier with France.

SUNDAY 13TH NOVEMBER 1938

Johnny Carey scores his first goal in his fifth appearance as Ireland down Poland 3-2 at Dalymount Park. Bill Fallon and the veteran Jimmy Dunne are the other scorers as Ireland gain revenge for a 6-0 hammering in the last game between the two sides at the start of the year.

SUNDAY 13TH NOVEMBER 1949

Ireland must beat Olympic champions Sweden today to have any chance of qualifying for next year's World Cup finals in Brazil. A crowd of more than 40,000 – the biggest for a World Cup qualifier so far – swell Dalymount Park but are soon brought down to earth. Karl-Erik Palmer, a frail-looking teenager from Malmo, scores after just four minutes. Peter Corr hits the bar twice – once from two yards – but Palmer adds a second shortly before half-time and Con Martin nets a penalty on 61 minutes. Palmer again restores Sweden's lead minutes later to claim a hat-trick in a 3-1 win.

WEDNESDAY 13TH NOVEMBER 1985

Eoin Hand's last game in charge of Ireland, who are crushed 4-1 at home by a Jan Molby-inspired Denmark in a World Cup qualifier. The game was also an international au revoir for keeper Seamus McDonagh.

SATURDAY 13TH NOVEMBER 1999

Ireland take on Turkey in a play-off for Euro 2000 in Belgium and the Netherlands, after narrowly missing out on automatic qualification. Next summer Galatasaray will become the first Turkish club to win a European trophy (the Uefa Cup) and in 2002 Turkey will reach the World Cup semi-finals. Ireland are missing a number of stalwarts, including Steve Staunton, Gary Kelly, Ian Harte, Mark Kennedy and Matt Holland but Irish fans in the 33,610 crowd at Lansdowne Road for the first leg of the Euro 2000 qualification play-off still expect a win. Ireland cannot find a way past visiting keeper Rustu and the game is goalless until 79 minutes, when Robbie Keane makes the breakthrough. But, Tayfur Havutcu equalises four minutes later from the penalty spot after a Lee Carsley handball, giving the Turks a vital away goal in the two-legged tie.

MONDAY 14TH NOVEMBER 1949

James Dunne, commonly known as Jimmy, dies suddenly from a heart attack, aged just 44. Born in Ringsend in 1905, Dunne was one of the first Irishmen to score prolifically in the English league, where he played for Sheffield United, and scored more than 30 goals in the 1930/31 season, including a hat-trick of headers in one early-season game against Portsmouth. He later plays for Arsenal and Southampton and is one of a handful of dual-nationals, winning a handful of caps for Northern Ireland to go with 15 for the Republic.

WEDNESDAY 14TH NOVEMBER 1984

Mick McCarthy and Kevin Sheedy make their debuts for Ireland in a 3-0 defeat to a scintillating Danish side in Copenhagen. The result is disastrous for Ireland's hopes of World Cup qualification.

SATURDAY 14TH NOVEMBER 2009

Ireland need a win in Dublin in the first leg of a two-legged play-off with France to retain a chance of a place at next year's World Cup finals in South Africa, but Nicolas Anelka dashes their hopes. The Chelsea player has cost a total of £68 million in transfers during his career and won plenty of trophies but has never played in a World Cup finals. His shot on 72 minutes would probably not have been decisive as Shay Given in the Irish goal has the strike covered but the ball takes a wicked deflection off Sean St Ledger. Given has no chance and Raymond Domenech's team, who had played the classier football without looking like winning, go back to Paris with a 1-0 lead that Ireland must now overturn.

WEDNESDAY 15TH NOVEMBER 1972

Ireland have not won any of their last 15 competitive matches, played under three different managers, and the last competitive win was a record five years ago – an unwelcome statistic that finally ends today when goals from Gerry Conroy and Ray Treacy give Ireland a 2-1 win over France in a World Cup qualifier.

TUESDAY 15TH NOVEMBER 1977

Brian Clough offers Blackpool £250,000, plus a player, in his attempts to buy Irish international Michael Walsh for Nottingham Forest. Blackpool want £300,000.

WEDNESDAY 15TH NOVEMBER 1989

Around 6,000 Irish fans are in Malta as Ireland qualify for the World Cup finals for the first time today. Two John Aldridge goals in a 2-0 win over Malta is a fifth competitive victory in a row for Jack Charlton's team. This run includes successes over Spain, Malta, Hungary and Northern Ireland with ten goals scored and none conceded. As of 2009/10, this record remains unbroken.

WEDNESDAY 15TH NOVEMBER 2000

The 2002 World Cup qualifiers kick off and Ireland make short work of Finland at Lansdowne Road in a game overshadowed by Tony Cascarino's admission in his recently published autobiography that he felt he was a 'fake' Irishman. In Dublin, Niall Quinn, Roy Keane, Rory Delap and Damien Duff are out injured and four others – Jason Gavin, Dominic Foley, Alan Kelly and Robbie Keane – are not getting sufficient first-team football for manager Mick McCarthy. With that warning, Finnan opens the scoring after 14 minutes. Finland do not give in but a second half enlivened by a streaker sees Kevin Kilbane score his first international goal and Steve Staunton net a free kick for a 3-0 win.

THURSDAY 15TH NOVEMBER 2001

Ireland are without Roy Keane for the second leg of their World Cup play-off with Iran in Tehran, where a 95,000 crowd see if Iran can claw back a 2-0 deficit. Two fantastic second-half saves by Shay Given from Karim Bagheri and Ali Daei keep the game goalless. As the match reaches its climax, Iran throw everyone forward and Yahy Golmohammadi does score – but not until the 91st minute. Seconds later, referee William Vega of Costa Rica blows for full-time. Ireland are in the World Cup finals. The Irish players mob manager Mick McCarthy but the BBC cannot use any of the footage, which is peppered with bad language. Back in the changing rooms, the players give McCarthy a standing ovation.

WEDNESDAY 16TH NOVEMBER 1966

Seven years after making his international debut, Johnny Giles gets his Shamrock Statuette after winning his 25th cap for Ireland in a 2-1 win over Turkey in a European Championship qualifier in front of 22,300 fans at Dalymount Park. The score makes the game look closer than it was as Ogun Altiparmak grabs a consolation on 88 minutes for the visitors after Frank O'Neil and Matt McEvoy had put the hosts in the driving seat earlier in the second half.

WEDNESDAY 16TH NOVEMBER 1983

Ireland record their biggest-ever international victory (up to the 2009/10 season) by steamrolling Malta in a European Championship qualifier. Only 11,000 fans are at Dalymount Park to witness the slaughter. The Maltese manage to keep the Irish at bay until the 24th minute, when Mark Lawrenson opens the scoring. Frank Stapleton and Kevin O'Callaghan also net before half-time. In the second period, John Bonello's net is filled by Kevin Sheedy, Lawrenson again, Liam Brady (twice) and Gerry Daly five minutes from time to take the score to 8-0.

WEDNESDAY 16TH NOVEMBER 1988

The Real Federación Española de Fútbol book Ireland into a hotel so far away from the Benito Villamarin Stadium in the centre of Seville that the team struggle through what manager Jack Charlton recalls as "hours of traffic jams" before arriving at the game. Deflated and frustrated, Ireland go down 2-0 in a World Cup qualifier. In his newspaper column, former manager Johnny Giles gives Ray Houghton, John Aldridge and Tony Cascarino just four out of ten.

WEDNESDAY 17TH NOVEMBER 1976

Johnny Giles has become Ireland's fourth manager in four years and today's opening qualifier for the 1978 World Cup in Argentina marks his competitive debut. Ireland had improved during the 1974 qualifiers but French football was stirring. St Etienne had just appeared in a European Cup final and a French XI including European Footballer of the Year Michel Platini, Dominique Rocheteau and Marius Tresor is too strong for the Irish, winning 2-0.

MONDAY 17TH NOVEMBER 1980

Captain Liam Brady and Mark Lawrenson are unable to report for duty as the Irish squad assemble for the forthcoming vital World Cup qualifier with Cyprus.

WEDNESDAY 17TH NOVEMBER 1993

A draw in Belfast today with Northern Ireland will be enough to take the Republic to their second successive World Cup finals. They play in front of home fans only after an earlier agreement that banned visiting supporters from this tie, and the earlier game in Dublin. "I desperately wanted to have our place in the World Cup finals secured before we played at Windsor Park," wrote Jack Charlton. "Circumstances contrived to ruin that ambition, and we suffered for it." The game is the last for Northern Ireland manager Billy Bingham, who describes the Republic's players as 'carpetbaggers' before the match. Steve Staunton is out. The rest of the Ireland side are fit but cannot make a breakthrough. Jimmy Quinn volleys the hosts into the lead on 73 minutes. Three minutes later Alan McLoughlin equalises. Ireland hold out for a point and a trip to the US next summer.

WEDNESDAY 17TH NOVEMBER 1999

Ireland need a result in Istanbul after conceding a late equaliser and away goal in the first leg of their final qualifying play-off for Euro 2000 with Turkey. The Turks had been sent to Dublin's Southside for the first leg. Unimpressed with the dire traffic on the way to Lansdowne Road, they get their revenge in Istanbul, despatching Mick McCarthy's side to train on a threadbare pitch at a velodrome miles out of the city. At the game, Ireland are immediately on the back foot after Stephen Carr twists an ankle and comes off after five minutes. Ireland dominate but Rustu proves impossible to beat. Turkey go through and the game ends with an unseemly melee and Tony Cascarino sent off after the final whistle for defending himself in a scuffle. "It is all so horrible, so undignified," writes McCarthy.

SATURDAY 17TH NOVEMBER 2007

Ireland sport a one-off grey shirt for the only time at the Millennium Stadium, where a late Jason Koumas goal salvages a draw for Wales after Robbie Keane and Kevin Doyle had put Ireland 2-1 ahead.

WEDNESDAY 18TH NOVEMBER 1992

Jack Charlton wants revenge for Ireland's last game in Spain, a woeful 2-0 defeat in Seville. "There was no question of us going to pepper them from the kick-off – that would have been suicidal – but I reckoned we had now matured to the point where we were capable of going after teams and showing our teeth in games away from home," he writes. Ireland draw 0-0 but could have won as a fine save by Zubizarreta denies Niall Quinn. Lopez is dismissed for hacking down John Aldridge, but a penalty denied.

FRIDAY 18TH NOVEMBER 2005

After a dozen years and more than 320 appearances, Roy Keane leaves Manchester United following an outburst on the club's television channel, MTV. "Just because you are paid £120,000-a-week and play well for 20 minutes against Tottenham Hotspur, you think you are a superstar. The younger players have been let down by some of the more experienced players. They are just not leading. There is a shortage of characters in this team. It seems to be in this club that you have to play badly to be rewarded. Maybe that is what I should do when I come back. Play badly."

WEDNESDAY 18TH NOVEMBER 2009

Ireland must beat France by two clear goals in the second leg of their World Cup qualifying play-off with France. After 33 minutes Robbie Keane rifles a shot past French keeper Hugo Lloris from 10 yards. In a heroic Irish performance, the game goes into extra time, where referee Martin Hansson misses a clear handball by Thierry Henry before a 104th-minute goal from William Gallas that clinches victory for France. FAI chief executive John Delaney says only a replay will preserve the "integrity" of the game. Irish Prime Minister Brian Cowen joins calls for a replay. France's Prime Minister Francois Fillon tells the Irish government to keep out of sporting matters.

WEDNESDAY 19TH NOVEMBER 1980

Gerry Daly nets a hat-trick inside the first 25 minutes of today's World Cup qualifier with Cyprus and Ireland go on to win 6-0, their biggest international win to date, with Michael Robinson, Frank Stapleton and Chris Hughton also on the score-sheet. When Cyprus make a substitution, the player removed sits down on the touchline and lights up a cigarette.

FRIDAY 20TH NOVEMBER 1998

Ireland slump to their lowest-ever Fifa ranking of 57th; just five years ago the Irish had been as high as sixth in the world.

SATURDAY 21ST NOVEMBER 1959

The Republic of Ireland take on the United Kingdom of Great Britain and Northern Ireland at football for the first time. The match is a qualifier for the finals of the 1960 Olympic Games football tournament in Rome and only features amateur players. The Irish travel to Brighton & Hove Albion's Goldstone Ground, where a 7,800 crowd turn up for the first of four qualifiers to determine who out of these two teams and the Netherlands will secure a place in the Eternal City. The hosts are weakened by the loss of striker Jim Lewis, a title winner with Chelsea as an amateur a few years earlier. Sonny Rice and Sean Coad cause problems for the British defence throughout and the game was 2-2 until the Northern Irishman Paddy Hasty nets a late winner for the hosts.

WEDNESDAY 21ST NOVEMBER 1979

A Gerry Armstrong goal on 54 minutes consigns an Irish team to a 1-0 defeat against Northern Ireland in a European Championship qualifier at Windsor Park in Belfast. The visitors are without midfield maestro Liam Brady but still force home goalkeeper Pat Jennings into a number of key saves but Ireland cannot equalise. The game is the last of the qualifiers and the result sends England, who are in the same group, to next year's finals in Italy. After the game Northern Ireland's part-time manager Danny Blanchflower decides to resign, having threatened to do just that once the qualifying programme is complete. In September, Blanchflower had also quit his job managing Chelsea after just nine months.

WEDNESDAY 22ND NOVEMBER 1967

Noel Cantwell is Ireland's player-manager but forced to put his full-time job managing Coventry City before Ireland's Nations Cup qualifier in Prague today. "Jackie [Johnny] Carey gave up the Irish job for the very same reason," wrote Tom Muldowney in *World Soccer*. "He knew he had a full-time career with Nottingham Forest. How then, one is forced to ask, can Cantwell, in his first appointment as manager of a leading professional club hope to cope where an established manager like Carey could not?" The Czechs need a point to qualify but Ireland recover from John Dempsey's own goal on 57 minutes as goals from Ray Treacy, then Turlough O'Connor four minutes from time, post a 2-1 win.

MONDAY 23RD NOVEMBER 2009

An FAI delegation fly out to Zurich for an emergency meeting of the Fifa executive committee over the Thierry Henry handball that has controversially eliminated Ireland from the recent World Cup play-off.

TUESDAY 24TH NOVEMBER 2009

President Sepp Blatter and the Fifa executive committee discuss the handball incident. Thierry Henry has even chipped in with his contribution, saying: "Naturally I feel embarrassed at the way that we won and feel extremely sorry for the Irish who definitely deserve to be in South Africa. Of course, the fairest solution would be to replay the game but it is not in my control." Fifa are in control. There will be no replay.

TUESDAY 25TH NOVEMBER 1947

Stephen Derek Heighway is born, the son of an Englishman transferred to Dublin on work. He is sent to a small private school in the Irish capital, where there are no organised games. When he moves back to Sheffield aged 10 he gets to play football and grows up a Sheffield United fan. His hero is Welsh international Len Allchurch. "I never saw myself as another Allchurch, beating defenders, scoring goals, winning applause from the crowd," admits Heighway. He starts playing for Skelmersdale, a strong amateur side on the verge of going professional but in 1970 is picked up by Liverpool. He goes on to make more than 320 appearances for the Anfield side over the next 11 years, winning league championships and European Cups plus 34 caps for Ireland.

WEDNESDAY 25TH NOVEMBER 1953

Ireland triumphed in their only other game in Paris against France 16 years earlier and must repeat that result today to qualify for next year's World Cup. Ireland play their part in a fine game but Peter Farrell, newly restored to the side through injury, limps off. While the Everton player is recovering on the sidelines before returning to the fray, Piantoni scores the only goal of the game on 73 minutes to eliminate Ireland.

SUNDAY 25TH NOVEMBER 1956

The Irish trounce World Cup holders West Germany in a friendly. A crowd of 40,000 are mostly happy with a goalless match at the break but Noel Cantwell opens the scoring on 63 minutes from a penalty. Last-ditch goals from Joe Haverty and James McCann give Ireland a 3-0 win.

SUNDAY 25TH NOVEMBER 2007

The draw for the 2010 World Cup qualifiers is held at Durban in South Africa. Ireland are in the pot of third seeds and paired with Italy, Bulgaria, Cyprus, Montenegro and Georgia.

WEDNESDAY 26TH NOVEMBER 2008

Ireland make their international debut at futsal, a short-sided version of football that is more like a mini-version of the real game than the more popular five-a-side game played in many parts of the British Isles. In Europe, there are professional leagues in Spain and Portugal. Ireland's opponents today are Hungary, who are ranked seventh in Europe and will host the 2010 Uefa Futsal Championships. Ireland's young team of teenagers and under-21 internationals is drawn from LOI clubs such as Bray Wanderers, Shelbourne and Shamrock Rovers. The Irish look to be in real trouble after conceding four goals in a frenetic six-minute spell in front of a capacity 1,500 crowd at the Miskolc Varosi Sportusarnok Arena. Ireland are not downcast and Longford's Alan Lynch eludes a Hungarian defender to become the first player to score for Ireland in a futsal international as the game finishes 4-1 to the hosts.

SUNDAY 27TH NOVEMBER 1955

A goal 15 minutes from time by Sheffield United's Alf Ringstead rescues a draw for Ireland in a friendly with Spain in front of a 35,000 crowd at Dalymount Park. Arthur Fitzsimmons had put Ireland ahead after just eight minutes but Spain had recovered to lead 2-1 at the interval.

MONDAY 28TH NOVEMBER 1955

Maurice Celsus Daly is born. He makes his Ireland debut in a 4-2 win over Turkey in April 1978 and retains his place in Johnny Giles' team for next week's game with Poland but after a 3-0 thrashing in Lodz, Daly never features for Ireland again.

WEDNESDAY 29TH NOVEMBER 2000

Chief executive Bernard O'Byrne has been given until Monday week to provide details about the proposed Eircom Park Stadium development, or face a vote of no confidence after a marathon management committee meeting. "The key issues are the funding of the arena, its projected income and the decision relating to the purchase of the site," says Byrne. "We've been over this ground a hundred times – but why not go over it again and keep everyone happy? The majority of the board of management supports the project, as do the majority of football people. I believe that we will be building Eircom Park in the summer of next year."

MONDAY 30TH NOVEMBER 1953

The draw for the 1954 World Cup qualifying campaign sees Ireland drawn with Luxembourg and France.

SATURDAY 30TH NOVEMBER 1991

"I suspect we will again be a force to be reckoned with in the next World Cup," reflects Irish manager Jack Charlton in his 1994 World Cup diary today after missing out on Euro 94. "I hope that I am proved right."

REPUBLIC OF IRELAND
On This Day

DECEMBER

WEDNESDAY 1st DECEMBER 1993

Jack Charlton gets off a flight from Newcastle upon Tyne into Dublin to be told that instead of the routine cartilage probe that the Irish manager was expecting key striker Niall Quinn to undergo, a more serious operation was necessary that has ruled the striker out of next year's World Cup finals.

SATURDAY 1st DECEMBER 2001

The draw for the 2002 World Cup finals puts Ireland, who are among the second seeds, in with Cameroon, Germany and Saudi Arabia. "At first glance, the game with the Saudis looks like it will hold the key," writes Mick McCarthy in his *World Cup Diary*. "We will need five points to guarantee our passage through to the second phase and it may all come down to that last game [with the Saudis]."

SUNDAY 2nd DECEMBER 1973

Graham Kavanagh, who was born today, is perhaps best remembered for scoring one of the goals for Cardiff City that knocked Leeds United out of the FA Cup in 2002. The win started Leeds seemingly inexorable slide down the league pyramid. Kavanagh was an established international before then, having made his Irish debut in 1998 in the midst of a five-year spell at Stoke City, where he made more than 200 appearances. He would go on to win 16 caps between 1998 and 2006 and after leaving Cardiff in 2005 featured for Wigan Athletic and Sunderland, where after a few loan spells he left in 2009 and signed for Carlisle United.

SUNDAY 3rd DECEMBER 1922

The birthday of John Christopher Lawlor. A striker more commonly known as Kit, he won a hat-trick of caps for Ireland in the late 1940s and early 1950s but never finished on the winning side. He made his debut in a 2-0 defeat against Belgium in 1949 and a year later moved to England. He signed for Doncaster Rovers and scored 46 goals in 156 appearances for the South Yorkshire club but the majority of his career was spent in the LOI with Shamrock Rovers, Drumcondra and Dundalk. He died in June 2004, aged 81.

FRIDAY 4TH DECEMBER 1959

Paul Nwobilo (later Paul McGrath) is born in Ealing, west London to an Irish mother and a Nigerian father but is given up for adoption at an orphanage in Dublin. He is just four weeks old. Although he gets into trouble as a child, his talent is immediately apparent and he starts playing regularly for Pearse Rovers as a schoolboy, and senior matches for Dalkey United, before turning professional in 1981 with St Patrick's Athletic. A year later, he has been picked up by Manchester United, where he stays for seven years before moving to Aston Villa. He later admits to playing top level matches while under the influence of alcohol but became one of Villa and Ireland's most popular players. McGrath made 83 appearances for Ireland between 1985 and 1997 and in October 1997 is the subject of a tribute show on the *Late Late Show* on RTÉ. McGrath arrived at the studios expecting a brief interview to find himself lauded by everyone from Jack Charlton to the Taoiseach. In his autobiography McGrath describes the experience as "humbling".

WEDNESDAY 4TH DECEMBER 1968

Johnny Giles leads Ireland off the field after 51 minutes as heavy fog means today's European Championship qualifier at Dalymount Park is abandoned. Finn Winnberg had put visitors Denmark ahead after 18 minutes. Giles levels with a penalty shortly before half-time but the game is not finished.

FRIDAY 4TH DECEMBER 1970

Leeds United refuse to release Irish star Johnny Giles for Ireland's next international, a Nations Cup game with Italy, as the game clashes with a European tie against Sparta Prague.

SUNDAY 5TH DECEMBER 1948

A goal on 53 minutes from Alfred Bickel condemns Ireland to a 1-0 defeat at home to Switzerland in a friendly watched by a 25,563 crowd at Dalymount Park.

FRIDAY 5TH DECEMBER 1980

As many Irish fans anticipate, France crush Cyprus 4-0 in Paris to confirm their progress to the 1982 World Cup finals – and Ireland's elimination.

SUNDAY 6TH DECEMBER 1936

Brimming with confidence after the shock thrashing of Germany two months earlier, Ireland are brought down to earth today by Hungary at Dalymount Park. Ireland had not lost for four matches and the visitors drop five of the team that had been pasted 6-2 by England the previous week. A tight first half sees Ireland only a goal down as Bill Fallon of Notts County scores his first international goal. Hungary increase their lead through Geza Toldi. Ireland peg the visitors back through a Tom Davis penalty and were denied another spot kick by the English referee Harry Nattrass as Hungary win 3-2.

SATURDAY 7TH NOVEMBER 1925

A historic day for Irish football as the Free State League take on their Welsh counterparts in Swansea, while the Northern Ireland Intermediate League travel to Dublin to take on the Leinster Senior League. In Wales the Irish draw 2-2 on a boggy pitch but in Dublin Leinster go down 4-0.

WEDNESDAY 7TH DECEMBER 1966

Ireland's hopes of progress in the third European Championships are undone by two first-half goals from Spain in the Mestalla Stadium in Valencia. Captain Charlie Hurley draws an improved second-half performance from his teammates but Ireland go down 2-0.

SATURDAY 7TH DECEMBER 1991

"Some managers like to attend the draw in person but I don't see much point in that," reflects Irish manager Jack Charlton on the weekend of the draw for the 1994 World Cup finals qualifying campaign in New York. "It is purely a public relations exercise and the thought of travelling to New York doesn't even cross my mind." Instead, Charlton watches the draw at the RTÉ studios. Ireland are in the second group of seeds with Austria, Czechoslovakia, the Netherlands, Scotland and Yugoslavia. As the balls come out, Ireland are put with Denmark, Spain, Northern Ireland, Lithuania, Latvia and Albania. 'A kick in the Baltics' goes one headline but Charlton says: "From my point of view, it's far from funny. Not only do I not know anything about the football teams of Latvia and Lithuania, I don't even know where the bloody places are on the map."

WEDNESDAY 7TH DECEMBER 1983

The 1986 World Cup finals in Mexico still seem a long way off as Ireland are today put in a tough qualifying group also including Denmark, the Soviet Union, Switzerland and Norway.

SUNDAY 8TH DECEMBER 1935

No British-based players are available for Ireland today and four LOI players are brought in for their debuts in the team to take on the Netherlands at Dalymount Park. Despite the lack of British players, the Irish team is probably the strongest fielded in the nation's fledgling career as the starting XI has a total of 26 caps. For all that experience, the Irish concede a goal inside the first minute. Plev Ellis levels the scores soon after and Ireland go off at half-time 3-2 up as Fred Horlacher nets twice with a volley and header. In the last match between these two sides, the Dutch had produced a devastating finish and do so again today, stunning the 22,000 crowd with three second-half goals to win 5-3.

TUESDAY 8TH DECEMBER 1970

Ireland are thrashed 3-0 by Italy in a European Championship game in front of a 45,000 crowd in Florence.

SATURDAY 8TH DECEMBER 1973

Preston North End pay Swindon Town £30,000 for Irish international Ray Treacy.

SUNDAY 9TH DECEMBER 1979

Steven McPhail, who celebrates his birthday today, was a member of the promising Leeds United youth side that began to emerge in the 1990s. Although born in London, McPhail was briefly on the books of Home Farm before signing for Leeds in 1997. In seven years at the club, he made 78 appearances and was called up to the Ireland squad by Mick McCarthy in 2000 and soon made his debut until injury struck. His appearances tapered off and he was sent out on loan to Millwall then Nottingham Forest, where he flourished under ex-Leeds youth manager Paul Hart. McPhail left Elland Road in 2004 for Barnsley, staying two years before joining Cardiff City.

SUNDAY 10TH DECEMBER 2000

Steve Staunton takes a £13,000-a-week pay cut to secure first-team football by re-signing for Aston Villa from Liverpool. Staunton will now be on £15,000-a-week. "Gerard [Houllier] liked having me around the place but he didn't see me in his plans for playing football. I didn't go there to coach kids," says Staunton.

SUNDAY 11TH DECEMBER 1949

Noel Campbell, who is born today, was the first Irishman to play in the German Bundesliga. He started out with St Patrick's Athletic and made his international debut in 1971 while still with the club, only to join Fortuna Koln in the German Regionalliga West. After the club won promotion to the Bundesliga, Campbell won ten more caps for Ireland over a six-year stretch that ended in 1977, when he was dismissed within a minute of coming on as a substitute against Bulgaria in a World Cup qualifier.

MONDAY 11TH DECEMBER 1958

Chris Hughton, who was born today, could have been a lift engineer. He only played part-time in his first two years at Tottenham Hotspur as he completed his apprenticeship but went on to win 53 caps for Ireland over a dozen years. On making his international debut in 1980, he became the first black player to play for Ireland. He first played for Spurs as an 18-year-old and was initially a winger but turned into a fine full-back, who amassed nearly 300 first XI appearances for Spurs over 13 years and played all three Irish games at Euro 1988. He left Spurs in 1990, played briefly for West Ham United and Brentford then retired at 34 to coach. He was caretaker manager at Spurs and Newcastle United before taking the St James' Park job full-time in 2009 and leading the club back to the Premier League after the previous year's relegation.

WEDNESDAY 12TH DECEMBER 1973

The birthday of Gary Breen. His career started with Maidstone United's relegation from the Football League but later took him to the World Cup finals in 2002. After leaving Maidstone in 1993, Breen plays for a host of clubs including Birmingham City and West Ham United and wins 63 Irish caps.

BORN ON 4TH DECEMBER 1959, PAUL MCGRATH IN ACTION DURING ONE OF HIS 83 APPEARANCES FOR IRELAND.

TUESDAY 12TH DECEMBER 1995

The draw for the World Cup qualifiers is held in Paris. Ireland are among the second seeds and put in a group alongside Romania, Lithuania, Macedonia, Iceland and the tiny Alpine Duchy of Liechtenstein.

SUNDAY 13TH DECEMBER 1931

Ireland come up against a Spanish side that were traumatised by a 7-1 thrashing by England the previous week in north London. Five players are dropped for today's game, which is the final outing for Patsy Gallagher, once of Celtic now – at 37 – with Falkirk and a 35,000 crowd swell Dalymount Park to bid him farewell. There was no sentimental send-off as Spain were 3-0 up by half-time and routed Ireland 5-0.

TUESDAY 13TH DECEMBER 1994

Ireland's B team have a rare outing but lose 2-0 to their English equivalents in a friendly in Liverpool.

WEDNESDAY 13TH DECEMBER 1995

Jack Charlton's team take on Holland in the familiar surroundings of Anfield. The sides both finished second in their Euro 96 qualifying groups but as the teams with the poorest records they must play each other today in a one-off game to determine the last finals spot. As England will host next summer's tournament, the play-off is in England. Patrick Kluivert scores after 29 minutes, then again two minutes before the final whistle, to bring an end to Irish qualifying hopes and Charlton's time as Ireland's manager.

THURSDAY 14TH DECEMBER 1922

At the annual board meeting of the IFA, an agreement is reached to try and heal the rift with the new Irish Free State Football Association by sending a delegation to Dublin led by Captain J M Wilton for talks and a proposal for a conference the following February in Dublin.

SUNDAY 15TH DECEMBER 1968

Republic of Ireland international Eamon Rogers is one of eight Blackburn Rovers first XI players relegated to the reserves by manager Eddie Quigley after a 4-1 mauling by Carlisle.

MONDAY 16TH DECEMBER 1929

Arthur Gerard Fitzsimons, who was born today, was a product of the youth system at Johnville and would go on to become a regular with the Irish national team during the 1950s. He played initially for Shelbourne but moved to England in 1949, joining Middlesbrough, and a year later winning the first of 26 caps for Ireland. An inside-forward, Fitzsimons scored seven international goals, plus 49 for Middlesbrough in more than 220 first XI appearances. He later played for Lincoln but returned to Ireland and was inducted into the FAI Hall of Fame in 2009.

SUNDAY 16TH DECEMBER 1934

Ireland's first international of the season brings Hungary to Dalymount Park. The visitors have played 130 matches – Ireland are just into double figures – and the gap in experience eventually shows. Ireland are only a goal adrift at half-time with Dundalk's Joey Donnelly scoring. Substitutions are common practice in Europe, but only permitted for injuries in Ireland, and when the Hungarians try to replace three players at half-time, Irish captain Paddy Gaskins objects. Hungary eventually replace their keeper and one outfield player and run out 4-2 winners through two late goals.

WEDNESDAY 16TH DECEMBER 1970

In his first full season as a professional at Liverpool, Steve Heighway is voted one of Ireland's top sports stars in a national poll.

SATURDAY 16TH DECEMBER 2006

The FAI can continue to pick Northern Irish-born players after a Fifa ruling today. The issue was brought up again after Derry-born Darron Gibson played in a recent Euro 2008 qualifier for Ireland despite having represented Northern Ireland at under-16 level. The FAI welcomed Fifa's decision, saying: "Senior Fifa sources have confirmed to us that the status quo remains."

TUESDAY 17TH DECEMBER 1985

Jack Charlton and John Giles have already been interviewed for the Irish manager's job and Brian Clough joins the fray today after Nottingham Forest chairman Maurice Rowarth receives a letter from the FAI asking for permission to speak to his club's manager. "There is no board meeting scheduled until after Christmas but I have no doubt that we will be able to announce our decision before the end of the week," Rowarth tells *The Times*. Clough later applies, proclaiming in typically ebullient fashion: "It's easy enough to get to Ireland, just a straight walk across the Irish Sea as far as I'm concerned."

TUESDAY 18TH DECEMBER 2007

Irish international Graham Kavanagh still has a future at the Stadium of Light says Sunderland manager Roy Keane. Kavanagh has not made a first XI start all season and is expected to leave in the transfer window. Keane suggests otherwise to the *Evening Herald* today but Kavanagh, who has been on loan at Sheffield Wednesday, returns to Hillsborough in the New Year.

SUNDAY 19TH DECEMBER 1993

Will Ireland be dealt a good hand when the draw for the group stages of the 1994 World Cup is held in Las Vegas? Jack Charlton eschews a trip to Vegas for a function with Opel at the American Embassy in Dublin. Instead of being flush with a good hand, Charlton sees Ireland pitted with Mexico, Italy and Norway in the group of death that haunts every World Cup finals. Ireland will open their campaign against Italy on June 18th at the Giants Stadium in New Jersey. "There couldn't be a much tougher opening assignment than that; but oddly I was not too unhappy about it," wrote Charlton two days later.

WEDNESDAY 20TH DECEMBER 2000

Could Ray Scott – better known as the voice of Network 2's *Soccer Show* – one day emulate Brian Kerr? Today, Scott is taking over as full-time administrator of the Football Association of Irish Schools (FAIS) with responsibility for promotion and sponsorship. Previously a teacher in Tramore, Scott has been secretary of the Munster Branch of FAIS since 1996.

THURSDAY 21st DECEMBER 2000

Robbie Keane joins Leeds United on loan until the end of the season after being unable to hold down a starting place at Inter Milan. "As a plc, we have a duty to our shareholders to ensure that we manage our resources with maximum efficiency," says Leeds chairman Peter Ridsdale. "After the £18 million signing of Rio Ferdinand, we felt it imprudent to spend another £12 million immediately – but by structuring a loan formula we have the player we want now without impacting on our financial position. There was a huge amount of interest in Robbie and it is to their credit that they asked him as to his preference and we are delighted he chose Leeds."

FRIDAY 22nd DECEMBER 2000

Fan power keeps Irish under-21 player Mark McKeever at Sheffield Wednesday. Bristol Rovers were on the verge of signing McKeever for £100,000 but disgruntled fans besiege the Owls manager Paul Jewell and the club's chairman with faxes and emails, prompting today's about-turn on McKeever's future.

MONDAY 23rd DECEMBER 1929

If Everton had not gone on a pre-season tour of Ireland in 1949, Daniel Christopher Donovan – better known as Don, and born today – might never have gone to Merseyside. Donovan was playing for Maymount Rovers in an amateur cup tie which Everton manager Cliff Britton decided to take in. Impressed, Britton signs Donovan in 1951 and he goes on to make more than 180 appearances for the Goodison Park outfit. The first of five caps for Ireland comes in 1955 against Norway and he features three more times that year. His next cap is against England in 1957 and after a 5-1 hiding, he never plays again.

TUESDAY 24th DECEMBER 1963

Born today, Chris Morris was planning to become a physical education teacher until Jack Charlton signed the full-back for Sheffield Wednesday in October 1982. He went on to enjoy a long professional career that included spells at Glasgow Celtic and Middlesbrough and also saw Morris win 35 caps for Ireland, during which time he played at Euro 88 and the 1990 World Cup.

SUNDAY 25TH DECEMBER 1977

Striker Glen Crowe, who came into the world today, spent four years in England with Wolverhampton Wanderers, on loan to Exeter and Cardiff City, then signing permanently for Plymouth Argyle but his total appearances for all four clubs did not pass the 50 mark. Born in Dublin, he returns to Ireland in 1999 and forges a successful career with Bohemians that sees Crowe score 110 goals in 180 appearances and win two caps for Ireland – becoming the first LOI player to win a cap for Ireland in 16 years when he comes on as a substitute against Greece in 2003 for his debut.

SUNDAY 26TH DECEMBER 1982

Born in Waterford today, Noel Hunt is the brother of Stephen Hunt and both siblings have successfully made careers as professional footballers in England and broke into the Irish national side. Noel started out with Shamrock Rovers before moving to Scottish side Dunfermline Athletic in 2003 and makes 80 appearances before leaving in 2006 for Dundee United, joining Reading two years later. His international debut came in a friendly against Poland in November 2008, when he came on as a substitute.

FRIDAY 27TH DECEMBER 1946

Joe Kinnear is latterly best known as a manager but was a fine defender for Spurs and won 26 caps for Ireland. Born today in Dublin, he moved to London as a child and made his league debut for Spurs in 1966. His first Irish start came a year later. Kinnear hung up his boots in 1976 and later moved into management, initially with Al-Sharjah in the United Arab Emirates, then India and Nepal. In 1992, he took over Wimbledon and steered the side to a sixth-place finish in the 1993/94 season. He also managed Luton Town and Nottingham Forest, before taking over at Newcastle United in 2008. After a dispute with the *Daily Mirror* over his decision to give his players a day off, Kinnear is recorded as swearing 52 times during one five-minute spell in a press conference. "It is none of your f****** business. What the f*** are you going to do? You ain't got the balls to be a f****** manager. F****** day off. Do I want your opinion? Do I have to listen to you?"

MONDAY 28TH DECEMBER 1992

The year ends with the Republic of Ireland at their highest-ever position in the Fifa world rankings – number six. Ireland will lose that position next year but clamber back up to top spot again in August 1993. Ireland's lowest ranking is 57th in November 1998.

WEDNESDAY 29TH DECEMBER 1937

Ireland will play as Eire as a new constitution that was adopted by popular vote on July 1st 1937 comes into effect today.

SATURDAY 30TH DECEMBER 1972

Steve Heighway pulls out of next month's game at Wembley to celebrate the entrance of the Republic of Ireland, Denmark and the United Kingdom of Great Britain and Northern Ireland into the Common Market.

MONDAY 31ST DECEMBER 2007

Lansdowne Road, the home of so many fine Irish international football performances over the years, closes down today ahead of rebuilding work. The ground takes its name from the nearby road, which is named after the Marquess of Lansdowne. In early 2007, the stadium is demolished and the new home for Irish international football re-opens in 2010 as the Aviva Arena.

REFERENCES

BOOKS

Back From The Brink
by Paul McGrath (Arrow 2007)

End To End Stuff
by Les Scott (Bantam Press 2008)

Freestaters: The Republic of Ireland Soccer Team 1921-1939
by Donal Cullen (Desert Island Books 2007)

Football Association of Ireland – 75 Years
by Peter Byrne (Sportsworld 1996)

Full time: the secret life of Tony Cascarino
by Paul Kimmage (Simon & Schuster 2000)

GB United?
by Steve Menary (Pitch Publishing 2010)

Gifted In Green
by Adam Ward (Hamlyn 1999)

Jack Charlton's American World Cup Diary
by Jack Charlton with Peter Byrne (Sidgwick & Jackson 1994)

Jack Charlton – the autobiography
by Jack Charlton with Peter Byrne (Partridge Press 1996)

Keane – the autobiography
by Roy Keane with Eamon Dunphy (Penguin 2002)

Liverpool: My Team
by Steve Heighway (Souvenir Press 1977)

Mick McCarthy – Ireland's World Cup 2002
by Mick McCarthy with Cathal Devan (Simon & Schuster 2002)

Rothmans Football Year Book (Various editions)

The Book of Football Quotations
by Peter Ball & Phil Shaw (Stanley Paul 1989)

The Complete Republic of Ireland FC 1926-2008
by Bill Samuel (Soccer Books 2009)

The Sunday Times Illustrated History of Football
by Chris Nawrat & Steve Hutchings (Hamlyn 1997)

The Team That Jack Built
by Paul Rowan (Mainstream 1994)

Viva! Ireland Goes To Italy
by Eoghan Corry (Poolbeg Press 1990)

Wembley – The Complete Record 1923-2000
by Glen Isherwood (SportsBooks 2006)
World Cup Diary
by Niall Quinn (New Island 2004)

NEWSPAPERS/MAGAZINES

Irish Independent
Irish Times
Soccer History
The Guardian
The Independent
The Observer
The Times
World Soccer

WEBSITES

www.englandfootballonline.com
www.thefa.com – Football Association
www.fai.ie – Football Association of Ireland
www.irelandinformationguide.com
www.kickinmagazine.ie – *Kickin'* magazine
www.kiltimagh.net
www.liverpoolfc.tv
www.rissc.org – Republic of Ireland Soccer Supporters Club (London)
www.rsssf.com – The Rec.Sport.Soccer Statistics Foundation
www.rte.ie – RTÉ
www.rugbyfootballhistory.com
www.news.sky.com – Sky News Online
www.soccer-ireland.com
www.thesportreview.com
www.worldsoccer.com
www.uefa.com
www.wsc.co.uk – When Saturday Comes